Love and Communication

Love and
Communication

Paddy Scannell

polity

First published in 2021 by Polity Press

Polity Press
65 Bridge Street
Cambridge CB2 1UR, UK

Polity Press
101 Station Landing
Suite 300
Medford, MA 02155, USA

ISBN-13: 978-1-5095-4752-4
ISBN-13: 978-1-5095-4753-1(pb)

A catalogue record for this book is available from the British Library.

Library of Congress Cataloging-in-Publication Data

Names: Scannell, Paddy, author.
Title: Love and communication / Paddy Scannell.
Description: Cambridge, UK ; Medford, MA : Polity Press, 2021. | Includes
  bibliographical references. | Summary: "An intriguing philosophical
  inquiry into the connection between communication, religion and love"--
  Provided by publisher.
Identifiers: LCCN 2020055611 (print) | LCCN 2020055612 (ebook) | ISBN
  9781509547524 (hardback) | ISBN 9781509547531 (paperback) | ISBN
  9781509547548 (epub) | ISBN 9781509549207 (pdf)
Subjects: LCSH: Communication--Philosophy. | Communication--Social aspects.
  | Communication--Religious aspects. | Love.
Classification: LCC P91 .S296 2021 (print) | LCC P91 (ebook) | DDC
  302.201--dc23
LC record available at https://lccn.loc.gov/2020055611
LC ebook record available at https://lccn.loc.gov/2020055612

Typeset in 11 on 14 pt Sabon by
Servis Filmsetting Ltd, Stockport, Cheshire
Printed and bound in Great Britain by TJ Books Ltd, Padstow, Cornwall

For further information on Polity, visit our website: politybooks.com

Contents

Introduction

This is the final volume in a trilogy that I planned years ago, as I worked out the books I wanted to write. And I should say (it seemed obvious then, and I did not need to mention it) that I meant *academic* books about the field I worked in: communication or media studies. The first, *Media and Communication* (Scannell 2020 [2007]) was a textbook pitched at advanced under-graduate and graduate students, in which I laid out the academic development of the field itself in the last century, in North America, the United Kingdom and (partially) Europe. I followed it with *Television and the Meaning of "Live"* (2014), written for colleagues as an historically informed theoretical account of live televi-sion. Subsequently, as time and I were getting on a bit, I retired from academic life and began to think about the final book I proposed, back in 2007, in the preface to the first book. Each stands on its own legs, and is independent of the others. But if you were to read them all (I'm not saying you should), you would see there is a continuum to them. *Love and Communication* was the title I came up with for this final volume long before I ever got round to writing it. I knew that I wanted to write about this at least twenty years ago, but when I eventually started work on it, both the world and I had changed, and I found myself writing something rather different from what I first intended. There is a time for everything, as Ecclesiastes and others – Karl Ove Knausgaard (2004) for instance, point out – and I instinctively felt that love and communication were matters best left until my academic career was over.

I

Being an academic was something that, at the time, I took entirely for granted, but as I got older, I felt an increasing tension between my academic self (me the professor) and my human self (the me-that-I-am, the nonacademic self, a usual person like everyone else). And this tension between my institutional and noninstitutional self runs right through this book. I took the title from a longish review essay, "Love and communication," that I wrote in 2005 about *Speaking into the Air* by John Durham Peters (1999). This was and is a book I deeply admire, and especially because it unashamedly brought religious thought into the usual thinking of the academic field I worked in. At that time, it was preoccupied with the politics of communication, the media as cultures of power, and so on. Peters's book was different. It was focused on religious and philosophical thought in relation to communication, and particularly communication as love, and divine and human versions of it: the difference, as he puts it, between *agape* and *eros*. He takes Jesus and Socrates as two paradigm figures who express this difference – Jesus and divine love, Socrates and human love. Their distinctive forms of communication capture the difference between agape and eros.

Socrates to this day is known as a talker, whose mode of philosophizing was dialogue. He famously preferred speech over writing, as Plato (who wrote his dialogue) made clear in what is known as the *Phaedrus*. As a communicative method it is quite distinct from that of Jesus, whose manner of speaking was exemplified in the parable of the sower. It was a parable about parables, Jesus's own justification of his method as a communicator. In this story (as written down by his followers), Jesus speaks to a multitude (a mass of people) by the lake of Galilee. Two different approaches to communication. Socrates goes for talk between two people in each other's presence (the young Phaedrus, and himself) – talk as dialogue. Jesus speaks as one to many – talk as teaching – and it is a one-way, not a two-way process. These two modes of communication are distinguished as insemination (Socrates) and dissemination (Jesus). We, I supposed, naturally prefer two-way over one-way communication. It seems more personal, more genuine, and authentic than one-to-many discourse. But Peters prefers the latter: dissemination over insemination. I had never thought of it this way, but it is surely right. One-way communication is, by definition, nonreciprocal. And in this sense, it is like agape, the love of God, who "gives" without any expectation of thanks and recognition. This for me was a trope for public service broadcasting. The BBC, whose beginnings I had studied in detail, was exemplary (Scannell and Cardiff 1991). In Britain, radio and television were and remain *broadcasting* institutions. It is a one-to-many communicative system, in which the apparatus "speaks" and multitudes listen and watch. They do not engage in argument. They are not obliged to take heed. The indiscriminate scatter of broadcasting, as in the sowing of seed in the parable, goes everywhere. It is for anyone and everyone, not just some. Insemination (the planting of seed in another) is for the chosen ones, but not radio or television, who began the process of full, democratic, communicative inclusion.

Broadcast radio and television defined (communicatively speaking) the twentieth century and, not by coincidence, their development ran in parallel with the full emergence of a certain version of politics (liberal democracy). This inclusiveness (all in, no one left outside the tent) is the basis of broadcasting. And like the love of God, it is one-way or one-to-many, and nonreciprocal. In what follows, I hold to Peters's line that there are two kinds of love, divine and human, agape and eros. And each is a different kind of communication. They come together in the end, but the start of the journey lies elsewhere. It reminds me of the old joke about the Englishman lost in the back of beyond in Ireland, trying to find his way to Dublin. He asks a local for help. There is a pause, while the local thinks it over before saying, finally, "Well I wouldn't start from here." The local was right, but you have to start from somewhere, and I must clear up some motifs that run through what follows before finally reaching my Dublin. I kick off with human and nonhuman interaction, followed by speech and writing. My goal is the love of God, and everything that follows is working toward this.

———

4

II

God, whoever or whatever that may be, is not some kind of *Übermensch* or super human. The everlasting virtue of this placeholder word is that it prevents me from falling into human hubris. Man is just *not* (even allowing for its sexist implications) the measure of all things. "God" is the placeholder for a power that far surpasses my limited, fallible, human, understanding. For purely human reasons, I will think of Him as some kind of "almighty father," because I cannot imagine any other way of thinking about Him and His world. But put this way, it draws attention to two quite distinct worlds: the divine and the human. With this in mind, I follow the Genesis narrative in which our first parents were cast out of the Edenic garden where they were naked and unashamed, and lived directly in the presence of God, and spoke with Him. Their expulsion from God's presence was, as the story goes, because Eve and Adam "were tempted" by the fruit of the tree of knowledge. For the sake of knowledge, they were willing to lose paradise, or heavenly bliss. I don't mean this literally, but neither do I mean it metaphorically. I simply take it as expressing essential human truth. Whether it is fact or fiction is, for me, neither here nor there. Leaving Eden was a deliberate choice by our "first parents" to live in a human world, rather than in God's. It was *the* original sin, in which human beings began to take responsibility for the world, rather than leaving it to God. What followed from this, over many, many centuries, was the evolution into history of the totally human world in which we live today. And this is the point of the distinction. Today's world (and we take it utterly for granted) was made by human beings, for exclusive human use. God was thought of once as the Creator of all life, of the living world in all its parts, including us. But now, we who live in our human world have no time for the rest of the living world and its Creator. We no longer share it with other nonhuman living creatures. We think of this "external" world as Nature, and it belongs to the natural sciences, if it belongs to us at all. We talk of the external world as external to inner mental life, but really the external world belongs to God and His creation. Leaving that world for our own was the original sin.

III

These two worlds, the human and the divine, are quite simply separate, and the Genesis story is an ancient tale of how this separation began. And this original sin (the human desire for knowledge) was realized in the *original technology of writing*. Again, I'm not saying it *was* the original technology. (Perhaps that was Adam and Eve's fig leaf girdles.) But the truth is that *our* world is wholly underpinned by writing, a very old technology whose origins are lost in time, like other ancient, yet still living, technologies – the production of bread, beer, and wine for instance. By writing, I mean the alphabetic system, but not just that. There are two written "languages": that of literacy and that of numeracy. Writing, with letters or numerals, has a long history to it. But it is clearly a human invention in all its stages, from the emergence of written inscription long ago, to the invention of the printing press, and the breakthrough into modern times and today's world. I do not mean to privilege alphabetic script (there are a number of them; this is Roman) over other systems of inscription, Chinese for instance.

These two systems of inscription (letter and number) developed separately, but together. We think of Socrates, Plato, and Aristotle as giants of philosophy because their works are still alive and well today, thanks to having been somehow salvaged, down through the centuries, by writing. And we tend to forget about Archimedes, Euclid, and Pythagoras whose work was also saved. Literacy has until today been the dominant system of inscription. Now, as the internet is taking over our world, numeracy is becoming dominant. Binary digitalization underpins the computer whose analogue interface I use. Writing divided the world into literates and illiterates, minorities and majorities. To be "unable" to read and write became a social stigma, and literacy became the highway out of this state; men of humble origin, like Thomas Cromwell, became powerful because they had literate skills. But today this has changed, and numeracy rather than literacy is the greasy pole to power and wealth. To be a functioning member of today's world, you need to be numerate because binary language underpins the internet, the horizon of the online world, and its various mediated forms of connectivity. Algorithms rule, ok.

I have had to rethink the relationship between speech and writing (Scannell 2019), and this for a number of reasons, but basically because writing comes *before* speech, and only with writing does language appear as such. I am *not* saying that writing comes before language. It comes before speech, which depends on language (but not completely or necessarily, and certainly not in the first place). If learning to talk is the *human*

Introduction

way of learning to communicate, we should remember
that species other than our own communicate with each
other perfectly well, to the best of our knowledge, and
some even communicate with us, and we respond to
their communicative implicatures. (When the cat rubs
itself against my legs and makes purring noises, I put
some cat food out.) But without writing, *language* is
not apparent. Writing made it visible, available, analyzable. We all know that writing came after speech.
Can you imagine language *without* writing? I can't,
and I have tried. The very ideas of "oral culture" or
"oral poetry," for instance, are literate back-projections
(McLuhan's rear-view mirror) that came retrospectively
with writing-as-printing.

Jacques Derrida argued, in *Grammatology* (1976),
that writing came before language. As he put it (at some
considerable length) it appeared paradoxical. But it isn't
really. It is, for me at least, the expression of a fundamental truth. My dictionary defines grammatology thus:
"The worship of letters; *spec*[ifically] rigid adherence to
the letter of Scripture." Religions of the book are gram-
matologies, and Marshall McLuhan is a grammatologist,
whose *Gutenberg Galaxy* (2011 [1962]) is a grammatology of the Roman alphabet. Instead of writing before
language, try writing before speech. The origins of language are connected with child development, *ab ovo*. A
child must learn its language, otherwise it will remain
dumb. At present, language acquisition is mainly studied
in the hinterlands of medicine (psychology, psychiatry,
child development), where it is taken as read that language acquisition is passed down from mother to child.
Unless a baby is taught by an adult, it will not learn to
speak the language of its parents, *Muttersprache*, the

language of the speech community into which any child is born. Without this, the usual child will remain speechless, or what some call feral (see the truly tragic story of Genie Wiley on Wikipedia). Linguists are prone to believe that every baby has an inbuilt LAD, or language acquisition device. I'm not sure I'd go along with this. I'd rather say we all have an inbuilt CAD, or communication acquisition device, and LAD is part of CAD. The point I'm struggling toward is the claim that speech, or preferably talk, is a universal thing that any child, anywhere, anytime *must* learn if it is to become human. And this is *not* primarily a linguistic process, although as the usual child acquires its *Muttersprache*, language (as talk) becomes increasingly important.

Any neonate, or proto-human, is inhuman. It is a tiny bundle of immediate needs that must be met (at least usual adults think so) by those who are its carers. It is learning stuff from day one. But what is it learning, if not how eventually to become a usual adult,[1] like everyone else? Learning this is *not* just learning a *Muttersprache*, their native language. We do not usually talk about learning to speak, though a child's first words are a great event. We say she or he is learning to *talk*. Talk is a term that I am overfamiliar with. I have been working on it for years, but you can work on something for a long time and still not understand what in fact

---

[1] "Usual" child/adult/human being. I use "usual" instead of "normal" in order (a) to recognize that there are "unusual" children and adults, and (b) to escape from sociological determinism (normal children obey the norms). In learning to talk, the usual child is learning (a) her *Muttersprache* and (b) how to be a member not just of society (which belongs to sociology) but of the human race. Unusual human beings are thought of by usual human beings as somewhere on the autistic spectrum. I regard myself as a usual human being.

you're doing. I have only recently come to see that what really got me going all the while was not media and communication in the first place, but talk. By now I have something of a bee in my bonnet about it. Talk is not an academic thing, and for a long time it was for me simply a taken-for-granted aspect of other things – radio, television, etc. (I edited a book called *Broadcast Talk* back in 1991). I *now* see talk as an interesting thing in itself, and I want to say that learning to talk is learning to be human, and acquiring a *Muttersprache* in the process is merely one aspect of it. Learning to be human is not a "language thing." Learning to talk > learning one's *Muttersprache* > learning to communicate > learning to be human. And the key point is that communication and language (both being innate and learned) are not the same. As we will see in the next chapter, the Still Face Experiment shows how a little child becomes a fluent communicator *before* she becomes a fluent speaker of *Muttersprache*.

IV

History and writing go together. One of the reviewers of the manuscript of this book wrote that "writing is a technological achievement, while talk is a *human* achievement." This is quite beautifully put, and I wish I had thought of it myself. I live in the exclusively human world, and hence I think of myself as a member of *historical* humanity, and God is not part of it. History began with writing, and this technology was invented by human beings. It made language *available*. It made it *historical*. In learning to talk, a child is not learning to write. That is what school is for; a later thing, where we learn our ABC. The skills of literacy have, for quite a while, been the basic infrastructure of the lengthy formal process of education. Mothers, or first carers, are mostly not professional teachers, and learning to talk is an informal process. Why would we let someone without any special training teach the speechless infant to talk? Because, as I see it, the mother is an expert in one crucial way: she is *a usual adult* and, as such, a usual human being. She is teaching her child not language, but how to communicate with adult others like herself. Learning to talk is a quite extraordinary skill, and it is ultimately about learning to connect with others.

Wittgenstein thought that talk was a primitive thing (Kerr 1997: 114); I think he's right that human talk is earlier than writing. But that does not mean that it is *primitive* in comparison with writing. Writing's telos is *not* communication in the first place. It is the first and greatest system of record, an archive that gives birth to history as we know it. It is a quite extraordinary human invention, a supervening necessity, as Brian Winston (1998) would say. Men began to make history when they invented writing. Systems of inscription made civilization possible if, like me, you follow Harold Innis (1964 [1951]). It made the language of talk *analyzable* and made *analytic* philosophy and linguistics possible. And philosophy as we know it began with Plato's writings.

V

I do not mean to give technology a bad name, by thinking of it as original sin. In the academic field of media studies though, it *was* a bad thing, and went by the name of "technological determinism" (or sin by another name). Back in the day, the dominant ideology in our field was determined by cultural studies. For academics in that area, it was human beings who made history, not machines. But that was then, a different moment of historical time. In the post-TV era of today, it increasingly seems apparent that machines (particularly Turing machines) *do* make history, and the academic field of communication and media studies has silently adjusted to this. It is no longer possible today to think of either or both simply in human terms. Media and communication scholars must think not only of human><human interaction (or talk), but of human><machine, and machine><machine interactions as well. I personally cannot help but think of media and communication in human terms, but I am a creature of the previous century. This book could *only* have been conceived now, and is about today's world, not the century into which I was born, not God's world.

VI

What I am writing is a mixture of what you might call religious and philosophical thinking, the new ingredient being "religion." Words are very rascals nowadays; indeed, they always have been: words like "religion," "God," "sin," to name a few. I cannot do without them, but they probably do not mean much to most people. I have taken a leaf out of Derrida's book (*Of Grammatology*), and will put them *sous rature* (under erasure); God (x), sin (x), religion (x). This simply means that I want to use words such as these, but I cannot use them innocently ("just like that!"), because they are almost drained of significance. And so I leave them there, in the written text, but crossed out. (Derrida picked up this useful trick from Heidegger who, in later life, would cross out Being – or Beying – as he wrote, but then left it, crossed out, there in the text.) Minimally, this technique indicates not just the hemorrhage of meaning from words, but points up their indispensability. I was born and brought up a Catholic, but long ago stopped being a practicing member of the Church (it was finally educated out of me at Oxford). But "once a Catholic, always a Catholic," as my elders used to say. They also said that it (religion) comes back when you get older. When I was a child, I thought that meant that when you were old you got religion again, as a sort of insurance policy, just in case.

This book is religious, but not in the "usual sense." I am not, as they say, a member of "a faith community." I try hard *not* to believe things (I most certainly do not think of the Catholic Church as a belief system). I do not believe in "the immortality of the soul," heaven, hell, purgatory, and so on – all the usual Catholic stuff. I am writing this book because now, as I head into deep old age, I find myself looking back and trying to make some sense of my life, and more generally. This book is an effort in that direction. I do know that the mix of Wittgenstein and Heidegger – both treated at first in separate chapters and brought together in the end – were the right companions for this particular journey to Dublin (maybe I should say Rome, where all roads once led). I also know, in my bones, that love, communication, and God go together, and I am more than grateful to John Peters for this.

I could say more (what writer wouldn't) but I'll sign

off with the little algorithm that the book ends with: f + h/t = love. F, H, and T are faith, hope, and trust (my version of Charity or Caritas).[2] These are, I learned as a child, the three theological virtues in Catholic doctrine and dogma. They are theological because they come from God, who has freely (unconditionally, non-reciprocally) given them to all of us. I am working my way toward this algorithm, as expressing, in a nutshell, what this book is (finally) about.

[2] I'd better say here that this is *my* interpretation of Paul to the Corinthians plus the Catholic notion of the three theological virtues, faith, hope, and charity. I have changed "charity" (or caritas, which I prefer, because the word "charity" today has lost much of its resonance) into "trust." I regard this as a very great virtue, but it is not usually thought of as interchangeable with love. That, for me, is the sum of the ratio of these three little things – faith and hope, which always go together, underpinned by trust. This little trinity of words amounts to an algorithm of love as I see it; either a divine gift, or a human, ethical thing. Or even, perhaps, both.

Part I

Talk and Communication, Writing and Language

I
The Still Face Experiment

I will start in a roundabout way, with the question of language, whose bewitchments make it hard to get at the truth. And what truth is that? What it is to be human, Heidegger's question in *Being and Time*. It is by now a long-established truth that what distinguishes us from the animals is language. But what does that mean? As I see it, there are two languages: one we all learn, and the other that only some of us learn on top of that. And to make this point is to separate language from something else, that something being communication. What every child learns is their *Muttersprache*, their mother tongue, the spoken language of their parents, of the speech community into which they are born. If a little child is not caught up in the pleasurable game of *Muttersprache*, it will not become human, and must remain a feral little animal, like poor Genie Wiley. The game in which the infant is caught up is not learning a language so much as how to talk. And learning how to talk includes the *Muttersprache* of her parents as part of the larger process of learning how to interact (or communicate) with an adult human being. This is the universal thing that every usual little child learns, *ab ovo*. Learning to talk is part of learning to communicate, as other nonhuman species do. Communication is not a language thing. It is not unique to human beings, and becomes species-specific for some but by no means all human beings when it becomes apparent through writing. All usual human children learn to talk-as-communication. Writing developed as human beings learned how to live in larger and more complex communities, and it became in the course of time a useful if not necessary device in the various complexities of economic and political life in large-scale societies. Writing-as-communication came much later in the form of letters to stay in touch with distant others, and later still as entertainment in the form of the novel.

I

The little girl and her mother in the Still Face Experiment (SFE) on YouTube (it has had nearly 10 million views) is introduced by its experimenter, Dr. Edward Tronick.[3] He leads us through the little experiment and comments on it as we watch and listen. In the crucial second phase – the "still face" moment – the mother turns away momentarily from her child and returns, at Tronick's behest, with an expressionless, motionless face that she

---

[3] The basis of everything I'm writing here is the famous Still Face Experiment (SFE), devised by the American psychiatrist Edward Tronick in the late 1970s. You can easily find the experiment. Just Google and watch it through – it only lasts a couple of minutes. I base all the points I'm making here as "proved," or better, *justified*, by this experiment, which by now has had nearly 10 million viewers on YouTube because it's so cute – in the same league as *Charlie Bit My Finger!* (For more details see Scannell 2019.)

will maintain however her daughter responds. And the response of the baby is the point. How will she handle the sudden (and inexplicable) situation she now finds herself in? Part of the fame of the SFE is that it is reliable, always producing the same overall result. The little child notices immediately the change in her mother, tries to reengage her, and, after failing to do so, bursts into tears. At which point the mother reaches toward her and reengages with her and all is well.

What is going on here is not learning her native language, but learning how to communicate. The child has *already* learned the preliminary skills of interaction with another as the necessary prelude to learning her *Muttersprache*. These essential *social* skills only partly involve acquiring language skills. They are all interlocking and equally important aspects of the multimodal skill of interaction: reaching out, ostensive gestures with hands and arms, face work, gladness of countenance, and blandishments. These were the things that were missing in the egregious experiment of Frederick II, the holy roman emperor who, in the thirteenth century, was convinced that the origins of language began with our first parents. And they, he supposed, naturally spoke Hebrew as they conversed with God in paradise. To prove this he conducted what is now sometimes known as "the forbidden experiment" (Shattuck 1980). Because he had absolute power, and there were no ethics committees back then, the emperor had newly born children removed from their parents and brought up by his court menials with strict instructions that they should be looked after in all respects but no one should ever speak to them. The experiment went ahead, but failed because, in the words of Salimbene di Adam, a monk in the imperial court, the children "could not live without the clapping of hands, and gestures, and gladness of countenance, and blandishments" (*Language depriva-tion experiments*: Wikipedia).

It is very well established in the academic literature (not to mention our own personal experience) that parents and others (adults and older children) talk to babies in a special kind of way. This distinctive *baby talk* is variously referred to as caretaker speech, motherese, or (child) infant-directed speech (IDS) – the preferred term in the scientific community. IDS has its own special vocabulary and a distinctive prosody. Its utterance and intonation are usually more gentle, in a higher pitch, with a cooing sound and "glissando variations that are more pronounced than in normal speech produc-tion" (*Baby talk*: Wikipedia). These prosodic features may be considered as the vocalized blandishments of *Muttersprache* ("motherese"). "Bland," *adjective* (L. *blandus*, soft, smooth): gentle or suave in manner; mild, soothing, not irritating. "Blandish," *verb*: flat-ter gently, coax, cajole; use blandishments. Note that blandishments/motherese are terms that say nothing about linguistic content but presuppose the *expressive* character of voice – a communicative, not a linguistic phenomenon. Adults will often talk to their pets in the same way, or to each other as a form of intimacy, or to other adults or children as bullying or condescen-sion. But in all positive instances, the blandishments of IDS are a display of indulgent fondness, expressively registered through voice modulation and other prox-emic devices. The parental voice of *Muttersprache* ties together everything that Salimbene di Adam saw as nec-essary for infants to speak their mother tongue: clapping of the hands, and gestures, and gladness of countenance, and blandishments. All contribute to the primary effect of shared, mutual, and focused attention on each other, as shown by the SFE.

Professor Colwyn Trevarthen has argued for "communicative musicality" as the basis of human companionship (Malloch and Trevarthen 2009). Trevarthen, like Tronick, is a pioneer in the study of child development and "language acquisition" going back to the 1970s. Over the course of many years, and across a range of related disciplines (pediatricians, child psychiatrists, ethologists, anthropologists, and social linguists), what gradually has emerged is a quite new view of the infant human child (in any culture) as endowed with, from birth, a *sympathetic* communicative competence (Malloch and Trevarthen 2009: 2) that is activated in interaction between an infant and a sympathetic first carer or mother. In his own work, Trevarthen has focused on the musicality of the voices of infants and adults "and how the pitch and duration of these sounds change as the infant attends to the habits of sympathetic older persons and becomes aware of the common sense in the talk around them" (Powers and Trevarthen 2009: 210). This work attends to the vocalization of vowel sounds by both parties. The word "vowel" is synonymous with "voice." Vowels are pure sounds; the breath of life; the utterance (expression) of "liveness," being-alive, life. Vowels are "key elements in the communication of emotion and meaning by sound" (Powers and Trevarthen 2009: 210–13). Babies are born with a powerful and delicate range of coos, calls, and cries, while the prosodic features of adult IDS tutor them in how sounds in the vocal stream may be shaped and interrupted by movements of the tongue, jaws, and lips. The upshot of this body of research is "that normal happy infants and their mothers use their voice tones cooperatively with 'communicative musicality' to sustain harmony and synchronicity in their interactions with each other" (Powers and Trevarthen 2009: 232).

A component part of learning to talk is the gladness of countenance of both parties to the interaction, confirmed by mutual blandishments. The necessary face and body work involved in this are both learned behaviors, but *how* have they been learned by the child (we assume, naturally, that the mother already has these communicative skills)? Not in any formal way. No mother says, "Now here is how to smile. And here is how to laugh." And she certainly never says, "Now here is how to cry." Her smiles and laughter *as* communicative phenomena are simply picked up by the baby on, as we might say, the way to talk. The encouragement she receives from adults when she responds with smiles and laughs at first are simply mimicry (they have no intentionality, no meaning content, but she is still learning how to respond to another) and at some point are subsequently transformed into communicative phenomena. There are things that are learned but not formally taught. But note how easy it is to say this, or that the baby just "picks up" communicative skills along the way to talk as if by some magical transformation.

II

The baby has not yet learned her native language, although she appears to be at what linguists call the canonical moment in language development, producing distinct consonant/vowel sounds (she twice says "da," while clearly pointing with her finger). What the experiment shows is that she has already learned how to communicate. Let us look more closely at how she tries to reconnect with her mother. She first leans forward and looks at her mother quizzically. Then, leaning back and looking upward (for inspiration?), she returns to her mother and begins her efforts at setting things right. She smiles. She points at something and says "da." In the pre-still face moment a little earlier, she had pointed at something and got an immediate, enthusiastic response from her mother. It worked then, but not now. She leans forward with arms outstretched. She claps her hands. Nothing works. Finally, she turns away from her mother's still face, wriggles in her seat and bursts into tears.

These are *my* interpretations of the baby's actions (for a more detailed analysis, see Scannell 2019). I say this, in the first place, because I cannot *ask* the little girl to justify her actions. She is not an adult. She cannot talk. I must infer her actions from her behavior, which I take to be meant and meaningful. As does Dr. Tronick, along with 10 million viewers of the YouTube video. We are all, quite naturally, able without any hesitation to figure out what the baby is thinking and doing. Dr. Tronick, as he walks us through the experiment, comments on both. At one point, he says that the baby "puts up both her hands and says 'What's happening here?'" She says no such thing, because she cannot talk. But in saying this, Dr. Tronick is behaving not as a man of science, but as a usual human being, who is "adultsplaining" infant behavior. It is not so much that the baby's actions are intelligible (i.e., meaningful, understandable, reasonable) in the first place, but rather they are treated as such by all usual adults. What the child is learning are the first steps in the arduous process of becoming a usual adult like the rest of us.

I would not wish to imply that the little girl's responses to her stone-faced mother are meaningless, and that we superimpose adult meanings onto her behavior. Her actions *are* meaningful, separately and together. But although they are meaningful, they do not translate into linguistic phenomena. There is a logic to her actions that we can infer from them. They are relevant, individually and in sequence, to the weird situation. What she does is not a jumble of stuff, one thing after another, in an arbitrary, random fashion. Separately and together, the component parts of her efforts to reignite the interaction make sense to us, adults. There is a logic to their overall strategy – getting her mother back on track. This logic is the logic of human communication, that distinguishes it from machine><machine communication. It is the non-linguistic logic of human><human interaction, that she is learning from her adult parent.

III

How would you explain – to try a little thought experiment – to the child what is going on in the SFE? Could you? I do not think so. The mother's weird behavior makes sense only to us, as usual adults, who endure without demur all sorts of crazy things that scientists (psychologists in particular) inflict on us and our offspring (Stanley Milgram comes to mind). To the little girl, the situation is simply baffling, and she does her best to get out of it. I do not think (and this is pure speculation) that she would be persuaded by being told that it all made sense as an adult experiment. She would think such an explanation was silly, or stupid. And yet it is the only possible "rational" explanation that could explain otherwise inexplicable adult behavior. The communicative, reasonable logic that the child employs could not supply the adult rational justification for it.

The experiment works successfully on infant (speechless) children. What if it were tried on, say, college students? Would they behave in the same way as the baby? I think not. The famous sociological experiments of Harold Garfinkel – the so-called "breaching experiments" – were designed to display the taken-for-granted character of the moral basis of everyday life. Garfinkel – the founder of ethnomethodology – wanted to show that ordinary social human life depended on a taken-for-granted "morality" in which meaning, intention, and justifiability underpinned all aspects of human interactions (Garfinkel 1967). For Garfinkel, a morally accountable (i.e., reasonable) person was one who could justify her actions in ways that another human person would find acceptable. It is in this precise sense that morality is the basis of a social order in which individuals are expected to provide accountable (i.e., reasonable) justifications for their actions. There is no use in an individual justifying her actions to herself: the justification *must* appear reasonable to others, and in this way the moral order is sustained.

Garfinkel got his sociology students to put a spoke in the wheel of the ordinarily smooth running of daily life by asking them, as a field work assignment, in the course of an ongoing chat with a friend or family member, to explain what exactly they meant when they had said something that was perfectly obvious, and to report back on the results. Thus, when an unwitting victim remarked, in the course of a conversation about the day's events, that she had had a flat tire, the experimenter asked what she meant by that. The victim's response was unerring and immediate: "What do you mean what do I mean? A flat tire is a flat tire. Are you crazy?" (Garfinkel 1967: 42). In adult conversational interactions, the response of victims to the experimenter's disingenuous demand for an explanation of the obvious was immediate hostility. They were quite sure that what they'd said made perfectly good sense, and instantly took offense at the weird request for an explanation. The baby is not offended by her momentarily weird mother. She does her best to rectify the situation.

The paradigm situation of the Tronick experiment presupposes, in a completely taken-for-granted way, a vast amount of informally acquired know-how on the part of the baby that it has been accumulating from day one. These include such other-directed gestures as the clapping of hands, and gladness of countenance. Many things are being simultaneously learned and refined. Communication is a multisensory thing (unlike our notions of language, always overdetermined by our literacy), and is basically what is going on in the lengthy, informal process of growing up. And this is not a uniquely human thing. The human learning process is much the same as that of other nonhuman species in which (as we're told in popular TV "nature" series) the mother bear, for instance, teaches her cubs the necessary life skills they will need for a solitary adult life. In saying something like this, we are simply generalizing from our own human experience of how human children grow up and into autonomous adults. At all events, what the usual mother teaches her young (human or not) are the necessary life skills for independent existence. The focused intensity of the communicative paradigm is, over time, diffused within the wider informalities of human family life. Learning to talk is the highway to adult society and culture, to being human in the usual way. It includes a spoken language, but only as part of something else. That something amounts to what Heidegger calls "being-in-the-world." The human world is both adult and sociable. To be in it presupposes sociability, and acquiring those skills begins at birth and continues through life. And it is not restricted to human beings.

The moment of the experiment (its specific timing in the psychological child development timeline) clearly shows that the usual child has become capable of learning to talk, *because* she has learned how to communicate. And learning this comes *before* learning the *Muttersprache*, as a prelude to it. I am not a psychologist, and my interpretation of what the experiment shows lies outside the vast bulk of the academic literature on it (for an overview of this data, see Mesman et al. 2009). As I see it, it makes plain that the experimental subject (the baby) has learned *how things mean*. This is a *prelinguistic* thing. The thing that has been learned, as the SFE shows, is how to cooperate with another as a meaningful interaction, jointly and equally co-produced by a usual mother and her usual child.

2
Talk and Writing

My take-away thoughts about this classic child development experiment are all about how to understand what actually is going on in it. As I see it (and my interests are communication and language), it is a canonical moment in learning to talk. And this means learning how to communicate, which in turn fundamentally means how to interact with another (adult) human being. This process, this multifaceted, prelinguistic thing, amounts to the all-important usual adult understanding that usual human actions *mean* something from the start. It is, in the first place, not about learning language – which comes later, with literacy. It is not that writing "invents" language, but it does make it (*any* language, part of its genius) apparent. It makes it visible, observable, and analyzable. In the past, only a few, a small minority, learned the skills of literacy. Talk, not writing, was, and is to this day, a human universal. Writing was not, and the skills of inscription divided the world in two: a minority of literates, a majority of illiterates. But that was then, and now, I think, writing is fast becoming a universal requirement, a "supervening necessity" (Winston 1998).

I

All children have in the past learned to talk as part of learning to communicate, but to be a member of today's world they must also be fluent in reading and writing, especially if they are to enter the new world of the internet, which is underpinned by *both*. The SFE is what conversation analysis would call "a member-shipping device." In learning to talk, the speechless little infant is embarking on the lengthy, informal, and complex process of becoming a member not only of her speech community, but also of the human race. What the child in the experiment shows is that she has already got the crucial nonlinguistic grasp of how human actions are meaningful. Her smiles, gestures, reaching out, and so on, severally and together – all responses to her mother's momentary still face – show that she understands these actions as communicative, meant, and meaningful, and she knows how to use them in relation to an adult other. *Because* she understands their meaningfulness, she can extend this to the vocal blandishments of her adult mother, and acquire her *Muttersprache*. Learning to talk > learning to communicate > learning language > learning to be human.

But what that meant was transformed by writing. I think of it as *the* technology for the simple reason that, without it, there is no history. As Cambridge sociological (quantitative) historian Peter Laslett writes:

What we have to recall, to reconstruct, to make a present reality to ourselves, is a time when most men and many more women could only think, and talk, and sing, and play, and till the soil, and tend the beasts, and nurture children, and keep house, and make things, like skeins of wool or barrels or ploughs or windmills, whilst only some could also read and write, and record, and refer again, and criticize, and tell others what was the truth of the matter and what should be done about it. Until recently history has been literally history, the record of men who have been able to leave written records behind them. (1983 [1965]: 233)

In *The World We Have Lost*, which first came out in 1965, Laslett argued that one of the fundamental differences between the premodern world (the world we have lost) and our own is the number of those who were literate and those who were not. The vast majority of men and women once had no need of literacy on an everyday basis. Academic history was invented in Germany in the nineteenth century and at first was about politics, war, and great men. This began to change in the mid-twentieth century. Only in the 1950s did academia get its grip on it, and began to discover other histories beside these. An early discovery was "social history" (as distinct from history-as-politics), and in 1955 a scintillating, and justly famous, essay, "The intellectual aristocracy" by Noel Annan, traced the complex web of interconnections between the literate, literary, elite English families of the previous century. Subsequent academic histories of women, nonwhites, and other hitherto ignored social groups (they were all "beneath history") began to appear in the second half of the century. Writing made both history and language *possible*, until the new media of the twentieth century came along.

II

Muttersprache (or talk) has one fatal communicative deficiency. The winged words of talk go in one ear and out the other. It is, by definition, one of the most evanescent of things, that comes and goes in the moment of utterance. It is intrinsically perishable. And this deficiency was partly overcome by the technology of writing, one of whose basic communicative affordances was and is its permanence over the *longue durée*. The deficiency of talk was at first shared by the broadcast media of the last century; radio and television were, like speech itself, ephemeral things that lived in the moment. As a historian of the parent medium, radio, I found it frustrating that no audio records existed from the 1920s when transmission began. It was, like talk unaccompanied by writing, prehistoric (Scannell 2019: 82–110). And so too with television (Scannell 2014: 128–52). The word itself, "live" (which rhymes with "drive"), took on new meaning in the era of radio and television; by the mid-twentieth century, it had come to mean the opposite of recorded broadcast material. The complex of audio and then audiovisual technologies came later for each medium. Without them, it was becoming increasingly difficult, if not impossible, to maintain over time a continuing flow of live (i.e., unrecorded) output. Without efficient, easily edited recording technologies, broadcast media simply could not manage to produce an indefinite and continuing stream of original output. The solution to this desperate dilemma was serial production.

This was painstakingly learned. In the USA and the UK, serialization and scheduling went together, as entwined necessities for keeping the whole business afloat. Serialization means formatting program content. Scheduling means formatting program output. Both media are temporalities. Time is expended both in making programs and in listening to and watching them. But, as Raymond Williams (1974) pointed out, the parent medium of radio, the technology itself, had no pre-existing content to draw upon. Right at the start, radio was a blank sheet of paper. When the BBC was launched, there was no content already there. The very early broadcasters faced a trackless expanse of "empty" time stretching out before them, which needed filling up with something to listen to, and later to watch. My first book, which I wrote with David Cardiff (1991), was (I now think) an attempt to show how this was done. It tried to show how "doing broadcasting" was learned in the BBC, and with what difficulties. I should perhaps point out that in the early "prehistoric" years (i.e., before industrial audio recording technologies came into use), the BBC's *written* archives were there with an abundance of material (all typewritten) from the very start. From these written resources, it was plain that, for some years, radio was a hand-to-mouth business, a continuing rush to feed the insatiable hunger of the microphone for something *new and different* for its rapidly growing listening public. But we have no idea what radio *sounded* like in its earliest years.

Let us presuppose that we have printing, paper, and books – the book being the first mass-produced consumer durable, maybe the technological break-point into modernity. Taking this as the baseline, let us think of language as *the* "written/printed" techno-system. Forget writing if you can, and then try and think of "language." I can't do it myself, beyond imagining letters, and words, and the odd sentence (all of which look, to my mind's eye, like written language). The ghastly impermanence of talk was the supervening necessity that led to the painstaking invention of alphabetic language. It seems to me that language (including the word itself as it appears here, on the page) depends wholly on systems of writing. It is an absurdity to suppose that our ancient forebears somehow invented language in the first place as a 26-letter (Roman) alphabet in their heads – no writing – and from there went on to put them together as an invisible unwritten language. In every conceivable way, what we all now think of as "language" depends on highly developed, historically recent, and continuously improving techno-systems of writing and printing (not just on paper, but now including an evolving variety of screens).

To survive in our kind of world, anyone must have fluent competency in reading and writing. Written language, everywhere, was always socially divisive, and historically dependent on literate elite minorities. But more to my point here, the association of literacy and writing overlooks that other system of inscription that is based on numerals rather than letters. Until the digital revolution, the undisputed language was the language of letters. But now the language of numerals has begun to usurp its authority. Numeracy is beginning to overtake literacy.

In the UK, the dominant academic way of understanding media was in social, cultural, and political terms. An alternative line of thought, developed in Canada by Harold Innis (1950) and his epigone Marshall McLuhan, took a long historic view that emphasized the formal characteristics of the media themselves and carved history into the eras of speech, and then writing and printing, culminating with McLuhan's view of the electric age of radio and television in the last century (McLuhan 1964). This was a distinctly minority view, and dismissed as "technological determinism" by most scholars in the UK. I have always defended technological determinism – machines *do* make history (Scannell 2009). Today the new galaxy of social media – artificial intelligence, robotics, algorithms, computers, and the internet – has overtaken radio and television, which are now old, twentieth-century things. All are underpinned by the technological infrastructure that determines their uses, their affordances. And these affordances underpin talk, technology, and writing. Innis, for whom both the spoken and the written were technologies, thought that their "communicative affordances" (their spectrum of possible use) determined the general uses to which they might be put in ancient societies. I am extending his thinking to today's world.

III

It might help to think of the SFE in terms of its taken-for-granted, invisible underpinnings, its technological infrastructure. It depended in all sorts of ways on the audiovisual tape-recorder to capture the interaction of the mother and child. But this was only the beginning. The experiment still needed to become available via the printed written word. It was only at this second stage that the experiment became available to its intended audience: a readership of scientists, worldwide, in the various branches of psychiatry, psychology, and child/language development. The very idea of the experiment itself presupposed that it was possible by the 1970s to make audiovisual recordings of human interactions and subject them to careful analysis via writing and print. This had hitherto never been remotely possible. The turn to the analysis of human><human interactions in the social sciences began in the 1960s when they became available for scientific scrutiny in some detail. Their platforms and techno-infrastructures remained not only invisible, but also neglected; not part of the experiment itself, merely their neutral enablers.

Perhaps the earliest step in this direction was taken by the young Harvey Sacks in the 1960s, who began to make tape-recordings of telephone conversations and then, with colleagues, transcribe them carefully into writing and print as analytic (analyzable) sociological data. Sacks himself, his collaborators, and his followers were all acutely aware of the fact that this process was more a matter of translation than of transcription. A decade later, as the video tape-recorder became a mainstream consumer good (owning a video camera was a very seventies thing), Edward Tronick was one among many in the scientific "community" who were turning their attention to human><human interaction as a newly analyzable empirical scientific phenomenon. But the same caveat applies. The audiovisual recording shows the interaction in more detail than an audio recording. But still, the process of translation (from one system of recording to another) cannot capture the immediate lived reality of the experiment itself. The clapping of hands, facework, and gladness of countenance, for instance, are impossible to transcribe, and very difficult to translate into the written language that thus far makes any analysis possible.

The analytic techniques developed by Sacks and others were unable (in principle) to capture the meaningfulness of immediate existence, but they did get closer to it and were able to expose phenomena that hitherto had been simply ignored. Their methodologies were scientifically reliable in capturing accurately such fleeting nonverbal interactive phenomena as pauses, however small, along with other matters, such as tone of voice, emphasis, and so on. Conversational analysis (CA) was able to show the meaningful character of silence in human interactions. Thus, to take a canonical instance, a momentary pause or silence in response to a speaker's invitation to do something together will be heard as a hesitation (i.e., intentional and meaningful) and preliminary to a "polite" refusal, the point being that this is *not* an interpretation of the sociologist, but something to which the recipient of the offer must attend. CA convincingly shows that a nonlinguistic thing (momentary silence, or "nothing") is nevertheless an intrinsically meaningful part of what's going on in usual social life. Data such as micro-silences are not linguistic, but communicative phenomena. And although audiovisual recordings make for more complex fine-grained interpretations of "conversational" data as a sociocultural thing, it is still very far from anything like a full account of the multisensory complexity of talk as a communicative thing.

John Peters (1999) has argued that academic thinking and research in the field we both work in has always stood in the shadow of work on what nearly a century ago was thought of as *mass communication*, and which later mutated into "media studies" (see Scannell 2020). I worked on the historical study of radio in Britain, and particularly on how broadcasters communicated with listeners. This came to focus on the question of talk, which, in the British case, was highly problematic. It is perhaps surprising, since talk is such a natural human thing, and everybody, but everybody, talks. But, until radio came along, all talk, whether public or private, was, of necessity, live and face to face. There was, of course, public speaking before broadcasting – in the church, or school, or at political gatherings, for instance – but talk in such contexts was direct, immediate, and face-to-face ("live," in short). Though public talk varied in context, naturally enough, speakers could see their audiences, no matter the actual context – they were looking at them. The problem for radio broadcasting was simply that speakers at the microphone did not know to whom they were speaking. Hitherto, there had been no such thing as "the general public," society at large. There were only different and distinct publics – religious, political, sporting, or cultural taste publics, to take notable instances. The general public only gradually emerged, over time, as the national audience of listeners to the National Programme, which the BBC introduced in 1930.

Talk is as old as the hills, but, until recently, it has always been part of "private," as distinct from "public," life. And, at the same time, talk has remained, until barely seventy years ago, unhistoric. The private (privative) character of talk is explained by its manner of generational transmission – i.e., from the adult to the next generation, as an informal two-way interaction between (paradigmatically) mother and child. *Muttersprache* is "learned" at home, whereas writing/language is learned at school. Talk was a private thing; writing, a public matter. I have assumed that talk is and always has been a *universal* thing, but that is not the same as saying that it is a *global* thing. The globalization of talk depended on twentieth-century technologies of communication that were, from the start, managed and controlled by literate minorities. This was not a simple process. The so-called "audiences" for radio and television were part of this expansion of talk that took place across the last century, by the end of which, broadcast television had become a global business with the English language as its de facto *lingua franca*. Of course, there are all sorts of qualifications to this line of argument, but the upshot of the manifold developments of the twentieth century was that everybody in a country like Britain could now, and for the first time, have a public voice.

But at a price. Control of radio and television rested with the broadcasters. Talk-in-public was not in the hands of private people, ordinary social members. Literate elites still controlled the airwaves. This only began to change when novel technologies (the computer, the internet, the smartphone) became widely available to everyone in privileged, rich countries such as Britain. The voice of everyman and woman is still not fully heard on radio and television, but it is on Twitter and Facebook. There is still a digital divide between rich and poor countries. But now the voices of those who histori-cally have been voiceless, who have been spoken for by others (children, women, nonwhites, non-heterosexuals, slaves), are increasingly being heard in some parts of the world.

It seems to me that the speech/writing dichotomy underpins not just radio and television, but equally com-puters, and what we all call "social media" (though all media are agents of socialization). The world we have lost could be classified along the lines noted by Peter Laslett (1983 [1965]): nonliterate majorities, and literate minorities, with all sorts of stigmas and privileges clustering around this literacy divide. But nowadays that simple and clear distinction has collapsed. It is no longer possible to define clear lines that distinguish, for instance, between public and private life (I mean, at least, that liberal democracy, which depended on the distinction between plebeian and privileged cultures, is on the ropes). And it is puzzling, to say the least, about how we might understand the impact and effect of social media – the puzzle being, for me, whether this depends on talk or writing, or whether this distinction too is under erasure. Is, for instance, text-messaging a form of talk by other means – with one's fingers – or of writing? Are emojis a form of compensation for the expressionless (still face) medium of alphabetic writing? Are social media a mix of talk and writing, rather than one or the other?

IV

Talk and writing have separate and different logics; the communicative logic of talk, on the one hand, and the linguistic logic of writing, on the other. For convenience, the former will be called Gricean logic and the latter Wittgensteinian logic. The naming of these two logics will become clear as I work through the arguments, but the starting point is the distinction between reasonability (Gricean) and rationality (Wittgensteinian). Reasonability is a universal, while rationality is not, being the reserve of scientists, and (for their sins) philosophers. The point being that the thing called rationality (and it has a privileged status in all sorts of ways in academic thought) is closely linked to language-and-writing: but it is only a certain kind of reasoning. I have argued that the little child in the Still Face Experiment already has reasonability, and she shows this. The thing that needs working out is what her reasonability *is*, what it means, how it works.

First, I assume that reasonability is a universal. Every little child has its inbuilt CAD. I naturally assume that other species have this ability too. Squirrels, from what I've seen, have formidable skills in working out puzzles set for them by human experimenters, when the prize is food and they're hungry. Reasonability is not the same as rationality, which is a highly literate form of reasoning. The way the child tries to reactivate her mother was treated by me (and Dr. Tronick and any adult viewer) as displaying a form of reasoning that is explicable in terms of Gricean logic. Paul Grice was an Oxford philosopher of ordinary language whose best-known work on the logic of conversation (or talk, as I prefer) became a founding text for the new interdisciplinary subject of Pragmatics in the 1980s. In working out his theory of communication (a theory of implied meanings in talk), Grice noted that it did not apply only to conversation. This thought is not developed, but it adds weight to the argument that Gricean logic is not, in essence, a linguistic affair (Grice 1989: 28).

In addition to the reflexive (interactional) character of communicative logic, Grice observed that, in ordinary conversation, speakers very often said one thing but meant another, and this he expanded into a general theory of implicatures, or implied meanings, supported by four "maxims of conversation." If we free Grice's theory of implied meaning from language, in the first place, it explains the logic of what the usual child does when her mother goes blank on her. First, she makes an ostensive gesture of pointing, which, by implication, is an invitation to her mother. Then she reaches toward her mother with arms outstretched, in the hope that she will reciprocate. Then she claps her hands, hoping her mother will do likewise. All three separate actions, in themselves and in relation to each other in that precise sequence of events, make sense to any adult viewer. There *is* a logic to them that any normal adult can readily infer. The child's behavior is about reconnecting. Their meanings are implied, not stated. But they are all perfectly reasonable to any usual human adult.

Grice's definition of communication began to show how this was possible. It presupposes speaker/listeners who can hear each other (a not unimportant by-the-way point). They do not in some magical way understand each other. If they are to "work" together in any way at all, they must communicate their intentions to each other (remembering that the little child cannot talk, but we infer – we do not "know" – that she can communicate). Right from the start, small living creatures have "reasonability," which is more or less the same as understandability. Both are givens, but they do not automatically kick in at a certain point. They must be activated, and that is what the mother is doing in the Still Face Experiment. It does not matter *a priori* whether the child's actions are "in fact" meaningful. The point is that *the mother's actions are meaningful.* Now we can see the force of Grice's discovery: an (action) is communicative insofar as it is meant to be recognized *by its recipient* as meant and intended. We share the baby's bewilderment at her mother's strange behavior because we make the appropriate Gricean (nonlinguistic) inferences. Grice himself does tend to focus on what speakers are doing in any situation. His is a speaker-oriented view of conversation. And this is certainly true of speech-act theory, which, as I recall, is wholly attentive to the speaker's point of view. The SFE belies such an assumption. The first "speech-act" is one of hearing something, not saying something. The neonate is pure "ego." Its initial cries and burps are meaningless sounds, and no more than this. The key thing is that, from the start, the mother treats everything the neonate does as meaningful in adult human terms, including cries and burps. When the child eventually "hears" what the mother is doing as meant and meaningful, *that* is the moment of entry into the (adult human) world. Hearing before saying, in other words. And mainly because, as Heidegger notes, to hear is to understand.

The mother is a usual adult, not a professional person. And she is, at first, doing what any mother would do, ordinarily, with her little child, and this is a universal "fact of usual life," like *Muttersprache*. "Informality" is a good example ("play" is another) of the great difficulty of spelling out clearly the meaningfulness of ordinary words. Part of what "informal" means is that it is a voluntary thing that is, at the same time, enjoyable in different ways for participants caught up in the *play* of the interaction, and involves the clapping of hands, and gestures, and gladness of countenance, and blandishments, and more besides. No one ever "proves" or scientifically demonstrates the meaning of the word "informality." And were you to use the word in the course of ongoing talk, and I were to ask you what it meant, you would, I suppose, be both flummoxed and angry, like the victims in Garfinkel's experiments. The mother "plays" with her child because it is the best way of getting across her adult instructions at this stage in the child's emerging life. But this rational, adult (academic) justification is superfluous. As we would ordinarily say, she plays with her little child because she loves her. And that is all that needs to be said. (This paragraph is indebted to Grice 1989: 171–80.)

I fear I am getting lost in the thickets of detail. I began with the question of truth, taking that to mean the truth of what it is to be human. I took this to mean learning how to communicate, treating this process not as learning a language, but a nonlinguistic process of grasping adult human behavior as meant and meaningful. The child in the SFE was in the early stages of the lengthy process of learning how to become human, understood as becoming a full-fledged member of *adult* human society; that is, capable, for all practical intents and purposes, of being at the same time independent of others and yet fully able to interact with them, drawing upon the same shared *Muttersprache*. Does this mean, then, that becoming human is tantamount to becoming a fully paid-up adult member of society? Is learning to be human, in the last instance, a sociological affair? I don't think so. Over many centuries, we have painstakingly created an increasingly exclusive world fit only for humans, and now we live in it. I hope the thought of writing as original sin is becoming clearer.

3

The Wonder of the World

I have been thinking about the two worlds – human and divine – for a while now, and particularly in relation to a talk that the young Ludwig Wittgenstein gave in Cambridge in 1929 to the Heretics Society. It adumbrates an underlying motif of this book: what it is to be human. The *Lecture on Ethics*, as it is called, was unique in several ways. It was not published in Wittgenstein's lifetime, and is his only public address to a nonacademic audience. But the key thing to note is the date. The lecture is often read as the first public expression of a shift in his thinking from the one publication that made him famous at a very young age, the *Tractatus Logico-Philosophicus* (2014 [1922]). This is one of those very famous works that everyone has heard of and none has read. Certainly not me, though I tried, but gave up after a few pages. I found it unreadable. Wittgenstein himself believed that no one could understand it, and said that, to grasp what it was about, all you need do was read the beginning and the end of it, which gnomically closes with the one thing everyone knows about the *Tractatus*

– its famous last words – "whereof we cannot speak, thereof we must be silent." He also said of it, in a rather baffling letter to his dubious German publisher by way of explanation:

> The point of the book is ethical . . . I wanted to write that my work consists of two parts: of the one which is here, and of everything I have *not* written. And precisely this second part is the important one. For the Ethical is delimited from within, as it were by my book; and I'm convinced that, *strictly speaking*, it can ONLY be delimited in this way. In brief, I think: All that of which *many* are *babbling* I have defined in my book by remaining silent about it. (Kanterian 2007: 85)

"It," being the Ethical, the topic of the talk he gave some years later when he returned to Cambridge, which he had left after completing the *Tractatus*. When that was done, its author concluded that, since it solved all philosophical problems, nothing remained for him to do in the academic world. So he disappeared to Norway and Vienna to do nonacademic stuff, and for a prolonged bout of further thinking. The talk he gave to the Heretics, when he returned to Cambridge in 1929, was on a traditional philosophic subject, ethics. If morality belongs to sociology and depends on usual adult humans being capable of giving satisfactory reasons and justifications to usual others for what they say and do, then ethics belongs to philosophy, and goes back to Plato and Aristotle for whom it was about the "good life." But what Wittgenstein meant by ethics, although it began with then prevalent academic, philosophical views, developed into something quite different. Ray Monk (1991), Wittgenstein's biographer, remarks indeed that perhaps the most striking thing about the *Lecture on Ethics* is that it is not about ethics at all, in any ordinary academic sense. Monk does not say what the lecture is about, if not that, but he does observe that, in a notebook written at the same time as the lecture, Wittgenstein wrote: "What is good is also divine. Queer as it sounds, that sums up my ethics" (Wittgenstein 1984: 3e). And that, for Monk, sums up perfectly the attitude of the *Lecture on Ethics*. In that, Wittgenstein puts it like this: "Ethics if it is anything is supernatural and our words will only express facts" (Zamuner et al. 2007: 149). This is in line with the thinking of the *Tractatus*, and its overall argument about language, logic, and truth. The supernatural (God, religion) cannot be spoken about. It shows itself in the world but is beyond the reach of words and language. However, the *non-dit* of the *Tractatus* (its unsaid) becomes the topic of the lecture.

I

But before I turn to that, I should say a little about its life history. It is a mistake, I think, not to know how a thing – anything: a book, a television program, a microphone – comes to be what it is. Any serious student of media, old and new, needs to know about and understand their care structures, the backstage, hidden history of how they were made, how they came to be that which they are. For me, the printed book, as read by anyone, is the end product of a hidden life history that preceded its final realization. It is obvious that no book (unlike talk) is eventually published without having been written and rewritten more than once, to produce a satisfactory "clean" version of it. And the publication process that brings it to public life reveals what, until it appears in print, is part of its hidden care structure.

I have taken into account both these factors in my discussion of Wittgenstein's *Lecture on Ethics*: how it came to be written, how it came to be published. It did not appear in print until after Wittgenstein's death, and only became an historical fact when it was published in *Philosophical Review* in 1965. In 2007, a remarkable edited version of the lecture appeared, with all known versions of it meticulously transcribed, including errors, marginalia, and photocopies of pages of the original penciled manuscripts (Zamuner et al. 2007). Though Wittgenstein was apparently not bothered about the publication of the lecture, he took pains over it. There is his first written penciled effort (MS1939a), followed by another penciled version (MS1939b), and then a typewritten copy of it (TS207). The version printed in *Philosophical Review* was based on TS207. The various versions of the lecture are laid out among punctilious introductions, interpretations, and commentaries by the team that produced the book. All treat the lecture as a philosophical work, and work hard to show that what Wittgenstein meant by ethics fell within the professional bounds of academic philosophy. Throughout, as an obvious given, Wittgenstein is treated as a distinguished philosopher who merits close attention by later epigones.

But who is the Wittgenstein who reads his written paper on ethics to the Heretics Society? I do not see him, in any simple, given sense, as a "mere" academic philosopher. And what is ethics? It is not enough to have information about the hidden production of the object as it appeared in book form. We need also to add the situation of the talk itself, since this contributes in a determinate way to what it – but what is *it*? – is about. Are we considering a talk, or a printed text? What is the relationship between the two? Are they in effect just different versions of the same thing? If so, we must privilege the printed text over its spoken iteration. The talk itself vanishes (as it must) from history to be replaced by its written version. The Heretics Society was founded in 1909, by C. K. Ogden – a Cambridge philosopher – as an undergraduate but nonspecialist, nontechnical forum, for Cambridge students and others (it was not a university closed shop) whose raison d'être was to challenge traditional and religious authority. Its many speakers have included Bertrand Russell, John Maynard Keynes, and George Bernard Shaw. The audience addressed by Wittgenstein comprised what you might call the lay public, whose members were well informed, but not necessarily academics (or philosophers). And this shaped, as we shall see, how he thought about his audience, and what he might talk about. I should add that going to a public lecture was a popular thing before the war (before television killed it off). If you were famous, that was an added bonus, and Wittgenstein was already quite widely known in Cambridge circles of those in the know as an intellectual wunderkind. I cannot but think of it as two different things: a talk of a certain kind, and a printed text. These are different, but they do impinge upon each other. And there remains the question of what it *really* is about.

The lecture (as a kind of talk) is not simply the facsimile of the written text. But what text? There are three versions of it, and I do not wish automatically to privilege TS207 (the public, printed version) over the two earlier penciled manuscripts. I carefully compared MS1939a with MS1939b, and found small but significant differences that helped to shape my interest in and understanding of the lecture as a whole. Edward Kanterian (2007: 123) describes it as Wittgenstein's "most accessible text." But I hear in that something of an academic put-down, and it is and it is not, or not in the first place, "a text." But, ultimately, Wittgenstein wrote his lecture and then read it aloud to his audience. He was there to do the talking. They were there to do the listening. And I am trying to "hear," as well as "read," what's going on in it.

II

Getting started on anything is always a ticklish business. Before he gets going on his topic, ethics, Wittgenstein makes some brief introductory remarks. They were read from the typescript (TS207) of the *second* holograph, which sets out an overall aim and intention that is very different from what originally he had thought of saying. Here's what Wittgenstein wanted to say in the normalized version of the *first* holograph:

> I feel I will have great difficulties in communicating the thoughts which I want to communicate, to you. (Zamuner et al. 2007: MS1939a-133)

He goes on to apologize for the fact that English is not his first language, begging his audience to make allowances, and to recognize that his *expression will therefore not be as clear and precise as would be desirable when one has something very difficult to communicate.* That difficulty being his topic:

When your former secretary honoured me by asking me to read a paper to your society the first thought that came into my head was that I would certainly do it and the second was this: I said to myself that if I had the opportunity of talking to a room full of people that *I would use this opportunity to say something that comes from my heart* and not misuse the time that I was given by explaining some scientific matter to you which to be properly explored would need a course of lectures or an audience specially trained in one particular line of thought. (Zamuner et al. 2007: MS1939a-133; my italics)

He then goes on to repeat that he would not misuse the opportunity of speaking to a nonacademic audience by offering a popular lecture, on logic, for instance. He continues:

I decided – I say – that *I should use this opportunity to speak to you* not as a logician, still less as a cross between a scientist and a journalist but *as a human being who tries to tell other human beings something which some of them might possibly find useful*, I say useful not interesting. (Zamuner et al. 2007: MS1939a-135; my italics)

The revised manuscript starts pretty much along the lines of the first version, until Wittgenstein gets to the difficulty of his subject:

When your former secretary honoured me by asking me to read a paper to your society, my first thought was that I would certainly do it and my second thought was that *if I was to have the opportunity to speak to you I should speak about something which I am <u>keen</u> on communicating to* you and that I should not misuse this opportunity to give you a lecture about, say, logic. I call this a misuse for to explain a scientific matter to you it would need a course of lectures and not an hour's paper. (Zamuner et al. 2007: MS1939a-179; my italics)

As in the earlier manuscript, Wittgenstein goes on to declare that he will not pander to what he believes to be one of the lowest desires of modern people, namely superficial curiosity about the latest developments in science. And then he continues:

> *I decided to talk to you about a subject which seems to me to be of general importance*, hoping that it may help to clear up your thoughts about this subject (even if you should entirely disagree with what I will say about it). (Zamuner et al. 2007: MS1939a-181; my italics)

These differences seem to me to be no small matter. From the first draft, it appears Wittgenstein's initial impulse was to say *"something that comes from my heart."* And this was then expanded into an opportunity to say something *"as a human being who tries to tell other human beings something which some of them might possibly find useful."* This is simply not the communicative intent and effect of what, in the version as read, he actually said. In the talk as given, the preliminaries are different. Wittgenstein offers his listeners a talk about a subject that seems to him to be important and in which he has a professional interest, namely ethics. What then, I ask myself, has happened to saying something that comes from the heart, and by a human being talking to other human beings like himself? Have they just disappeared as Wittgenstein thought the better of his initial thoughts? I do not think so, but my interpretation of the lecture depends on considering it as both something said and something read from a typewritten script. And furthermore as something that comes from the heart by a human being speaking to other human beings on first impulse, and, on reflection, a lecture on a philosophical topic (ethics) read to an informed lay audience.

The author is pulled both ways, as I see it, throughout: between a human being talking to others like himself, and being a Cambridge academic reading a paper on ethics to a lay audience in the hope it might clarify this important topic for them. The author of the *Tractatus* wrote a short book that claimed to solve, once and for all, the problems of philosophy – a breathtaking presumption that rested on a close-knit argument about language, logic, and mathematics. He spent the rest of his life arguing against himself, but never quite believing the nonscientific alternative. Or so it seems to me. All accounts of him, by contemporaries who knew and wrote about him, testify to his abiding interest in, for want of a better word, religion. As a child, he was brought up as a Catholic and overlooked his Jewish heritage. His views on organized religion, or Catholicism, seem banal to me, or at least very conventional. And yet his moral seriousness pervades everything he thought, wrote, and did. And this seriousness, which was second nature to him, is what I mean by saying that Wittgenstein was a religious man.

The final difficulty Wittgenstein confronted in his preliminary remarks was not just getting started, but indicating the road ahead, the topic itself, how it starts, carries on, and concludes. As he puts it, how *do* you explain a (philosophical) matter in such a way that the hearer sees at once the road he is led along and the goal to which it leads? He asks for his audience's patience, and hopes they will in the end come to see what he's driving at. So off we go:

> Now let me begin. My subject is ethics and I will adopt the definition or explanation that Prof. Moore has given in his *Principia Ethica* which is: "Ethics is the general enquiry into what is good." (Zamuner et al. 2007: MS1939a-137)

III

We are in, it seems, for a standard academic lecture, Ethics 101. Wittgenstein immediately modifies this slightly, saying that ethics is the general inquiry into what is valuable, and this because it allows him to include aesthetics – and the reason for this will perhaps become clear later on he hopes. That reference (to aesthetics) is omitted in MS1939b and TS207, perhaps because later on Wittgenstein never does get around to returning to it. There then follow several pages (in the printed version) of what J. L. Austin called "linguistic botanizing," standard professional philosophic stuff, culminating in Wittgenstein's enigmatic remark: "Ethics if it is anything is supernatural and our words will only express facts as a teacup will only hold a teacupful of water [and if I was to pour a gallon of water over it.]." The last bit in brackets makes no sense, and is punctuated slightly differently in TS207, but taken as a transcribed sentence it is meaningless unless you cut the last bit. The general direction though is clear, and leads toward what Wittgenstein, invoking the psychology of pleasure (Zamuner et al. 2007: MS1939a-153), is driving at. He asks his audience members to recall "a typical situation in which you always felt pleasure" (ibid.). What he then says (as it appears in print) is rather scrambled: "Now in this situation I am if I want to fix my mind on what I mean by absolute or ethical value." But it's a talk, and the meaning again is clear enough. He is inviting his listeners to imagine situations as common experiences, because he wants to talk about his own. And it is at this point that what started off as a usual academic public lecture to a willing but ignorant lay audience begins to slip its academic moorings, turning into something else.

Kanterian, comparing the lecture with the *Tractatus*, observes:

> Where the lecture goes beyond the book is to give a veritable phenomenology of religious experience. He discusses three such experiences, namely those summarized by the phrases "How extraordinary that anything should exist" (the wonder of the world), "I am safe, nothing can injure me whatever happens" (absolute safety) and "God disapproves of our conduct" (absolute guilt). (2007: 123)

I agree with this, but we need to clarify two things that are givens in the lecture. What is an experience, and are Wittgenstein's experiences "religious"? There is a difference between experience in general and experience in particular, *an* experience as Wittgenstein has it. In general, experience has, as its given content, life – hence "*lived* experience," the experience of being alive and living in the world. We encounter the world in, through, and as our experience of it in the course of a life (this is spelled out in the next chapter). It is against the pervasive background of ordinary, mundane life-as-experience that particular experiences appear.

The easiest way to dismiss experiences is to tag them

as "subjective." They are mine in each case, certainly, but that is not *all* they are. If experiences were *merely* subjective (i.e., uniquely, in each case, mine and no one else's), then there would be nothing to be said (more exactly, nothing sayable) about it. It would be a private and incommunicable matter that had no language to give expression to it. But evidently this is not the case. Experience *is* shared and shareable. There are many familiar kinds of experiences-in-common in ordinary daily life: the football game, the movie, the family wedding that we went to (or *that* wedding we watched on TV). These are obvious examples of common public experiences that we share with others. Of course, we do not all have the *same* experience of the game, the wedding, the movie. One half of the crowd at the football game has a good experience, while the other half (whose side has lost) has a bad experience. Wedding guests may have very different private feelings depending on their relationship to one or other of the happy couple. This is the dialectics of experience: it is very often, at one and the same time, experience-in-common and uniquely, in each case, *mine*.

But are Wittgenstein's experiences (which take up almost all of the talk) religious? As summarized by Kanterian (2007: 123), there are three experiences, presented in the following order: the wonder of the world, absolute safety, and absolute guilt. None of these strikes me as having much to do with ethics, as a branch of early twentieth-century academic philosophy. As he gets to grips with his first example ("the wonder of the world"), Wittgenstein tries to impress upon his audience that "a certain characteristic misuse of language runs through *all* ethical and religious expressions" (Zamuner et al. 2007:

MS1939a-159; original emphasis). Note how easily, how innocently, the word "religious" is slipped into the talk here for the first time. We are beginning to change tack. His first experience (*the* experience), to "wonder at the *existence* of the world" (my emphasis), is by no means the same as the wonder *of* the world, which presupposes that it exists. The wonder of the existence of the world is also shared by Heidegger, of whom more anon. I feel that to wonder at this is a pretty commonplace or shared experience by lay people as much as by philosophers. The second experience is perhaps more of a religious thing. Absolute safety is most certainly something I have felt. When I come to think of it, I find myself reflecting that I feel safe in God's hands or, as the poet puts it, "God's in His heaven. All's right with the world." (I actually thought this came from the Bible, or maybe Shakespeare, and was much surprised to find out that these were Robert Browning's words.) But the last of the three, "absolute guilt," most certainly describes a religious experience in a conventional sense (within orthodox Christian/Catholic doctrine and dogma).

As Wittgenstein comes toward the end of his talk, he marshals his thoughts. He looks back, down the road he has taken, and where it has led him. His talk about ethics, which began as an academic thing, starting with Professor Moore's definition of it, transitioned imperceptibly into one human being talking to others like himself, as he spoke of his own experiences knowing that everyone would know and understand them because they too had felt such things. As he works through them, they become increasingly religious in character, though what that means leads the academic in him to an ultimate paradox – the main point of his paper – "that an experience a fact should have absolute value" (Zamuner et al. 2007: MS1939a-163). As he was writing, Wittgenstein was parsimonious in his use of punctuation, and the transcripts faithfully record the error: there should of course be commas after "experience" and "fact." The same error occurs a little earlier, when he writes "that an experience a fact should have a supernatural value." Both transcriptions of the penciled manuscripts faithfully preserve this small error of literacy, but it is corrected in TS207. I'm sure that Wittgenstein as he spoke provided the necessary micropauses as commas. But as he initially wrote it down, I feel he wrote fast as ideas crowded in upon him, and the commas disappeared in the rush toward getting his thoughts on paper.

At the end of the lecture, Wittgenstein returns to his original experience, now described slightly differently as "wondering at existence." "We all know what in ordinary life would be called a miracle: it obviously is simply an event the like of which we have never yet seen" (Zamuner et al. 2007: MS1939a-165). (I must point out that "We all know" is a trick often used by all of us, not just in academic lectures. It is mainly a membershipping device to establish rapport between speaker and those spoken to.) Wittgenstein goes on immediately into another thought experiment. Imagine that someone in the audience grew a lion's head and started to roar. That's as extraordinary a thing as Wittgenstein could imagine. And once he has gotten over his initial surprise, he would fetch a physiologist and have the case scientifically investigated. Indeed, he would have the "lion-man" vivisected, were it not for fear of hurting him. Well I often find philosophical thought experiments silly, and this one seems pretty daft to me. But not its point, which is *where has the miracle gone to?* The scientific way of looking at facts is not the way to look at the world, existence, life itself, as a miracle. It makes no sense, Wittgenstein thinks, to say "science has proved there are no miracles." To wonder at existence is the same as the experience of looking at existence as a miracle. And he is tempted to say *that the right expression in language for the miracle of the existence of the world is the miracle of the existence of language* (Zamuner et al. 2007: MS1939a-169).

Pulling his threads together, as he famously put it:

> All I wanted to do was to go beyond the world, and that is to say beyond language. But this is just impossible. My whole tendency and as I believe the tendency of all those who have tried to talk or write about Ethics and Religion was to run against the boundaries of language. This running against the walls of our cage is perfectly, absolutely, hopeless. I therefore believe that so far as Ethics springs from the desire to say something about the ultimate meaning of life, the absolute good, the absolute important it can be no science, what it says does not add to our knowledge in any sense. But it is a document of a tendency in the human mind which I personally cannot help respecting deeply and I would not for my life ridicule it. (Zamuner et al. 2007: MS1939a-171–3)

The engagement with ethics qua religion leads to the grand finale of the miracle of existence, of life itself. Wittgenstein finally sees, as it were in a flash of light (a moment of vision, a Heideggerian *Augenblick*), that any attempt to explain the wonder of existence in words is absurd nonsense. It's not just that explanations belong to science; they belong to words, and language turns out to be the ultimate miracle, not the world. And this is where I part company with Wittgenstein and take a different road. For the world, not language, is the ultimate miracle, as far as I am concerned. But whose world? Ours, or God's?

IV

Religion (x) for the likes of me is a goner. And if God no longer exists, it is because religion no longer exists. They were once facts of life – as they were for me as I was growing up. The world once had religion as everybody's horizon, just as, today, politics is the taken-for-granted horizon for just about all. The adult me looks back to childhood and hopelessly tries to recover religion and God as the things that they once were for me. But it's pointless, like running against the walls of our cage. In adolescence, I came to the conclusion (in a flash, as Wittgenstein would say) that there is no afterlife, there's only this life, being in *this* human, historical, world, and we, adults, must bear its fardels. Hamlet (who makes an appearance in the *Lecture*) is right. The readiness is all (readiness for what? For my eventual death I guess). There *is* a special providence in a sparrow's fall. It would be a joy, a blessing, if my death, and the sparrow's fall, were noticed by a God who cares for all living things.

Certainly, neither is noticed in the living human world in which I live. And that is why I stand in need of forgiveness. And I prefer this, rather than Wittgenstein's notion of guilt. I do not think that individuals need own up to personal guilt. Sin is not to do with individual failings. It is an historical and essentially political concept that encompasses the sins of war, against other human beings, against other animals, against nature, against life. None of these is necessarily a human crime, but I do see them all as sinful. Sin is the marker of God's justice, as crime is the marker of human justice. Are slavery and the oppression of women, for instance, sins or crimes? All I know is that I obviously stand in need of forgiveness for the countless agelong sins of history, and in particular our sins against God and His creatures, the living world, the divine world – I can only hang my head in shame. And that is *why* I stand in need of forgiveness. I cannot ask for this, yet I stand in need of it. Writing was the original sin, because it led inexorably to the exclusive, human-centered world of today, in which I live.

The wonder of the world is a commonplace thought. Anyone and everyone will, in some situation or other, have had thoughts along these lines. But feeling safe (*really* safe) is something I understand in relation to the saying, "God's in His heaven. All's right with the world." Feeling safe! For me it means to be freed completely from anxiety. From adult anxiety, more exactly, which is a dreadful thing. Feeling safe is a childish – no, a childlike – thing. It is, perhaps, a more exact expression of how we, human beings, stand in relation to God. When He is in His heaven, then all is well with the human world. When I was very young, my mother told me that I had a guardian angel. Everybody had one, because everyone was special (like a sparrow) in God's eyes, and so I had my very own angel like everyone else, who would look after me, because I was special in God's eyes. It is not that I somehow believed any or all of this. They were just facts of life, like the world; and the world was a miracle, and I had an angel.

As I progressed in my formal education (at a Catholic school for boys) I expanded my skills of literacy, reading, and writing, ultimately going to Oxford to read English, followed by a career as a university teacher. And at Oxford and ever since, I let go of being a Catholic. But from infancy, and as I was growing up, my world was wholly Catholic, just as a matter of fact, and it was nothing else. It was the horizon of my existence. The whole of life. Being a Catholic was everything and nothing. Just a fact of life (mine). And all this, I think, is what the thing "we" call religion amounts to. It is everything and nothing, which means that it's very ordinary, just a fact or, better, a horizonal thing like life. There were miracles in my life because they were in the New Testament (a book I revered, naturally, but never read). There was the water into wine for one, and walking on water, and that kind of thing. It is surely obvious *not* that I *believed* any of this, but that miracles were, in my world, just ordinary, taken-for-granted facts of life, like getting up in the morning and going to school. Religion is *not* a matter of belief, and that includes God. He is *the* horizon, everything and nothing. He just *is*. But not in the world that I inhabit.

So there you have it, or at least you have a pretty good idea of what the lecture was about, and what I thought of it. My first thought about the end of Wittgenstein's road is a certain feeling of *déjà vu*. I've heard this before. Max Weber made the same point about running against the bars of the cage, in his celebrated description of the "iron cage" of industrial modernity, and the consequent "disenchantment of the world." The paradox of Wittgenstein's talk is – as he describes it – insoluble, and to the end he remains the logician, the scientist, the academic of his early famous work, the *Tractatus*. He'd like to be, he longs to be, a religious person. But he isn't. He's a modernist, a scientist, a logician, an academic through and through. That's what I think – and yet. And yet. What lingers in my mind is that Wittgenstein knows what he's doing is quite pointless, but that, I'm glad to say, didn't stop him.

Part II
Miracles

Part II

A Study

4
Heidegger's Teacup

I once wrote a book that I nearly called Heidegger's Teacup. I had written it I thought, but it lay languishing in the virtual reality of my laptop for nearly a year because I could not see how to finish it. I kept writing and rewriting the last chapter, getting nowhere (Scannell 2014). Eventually I saw that I had in fact finished it, and that what it really needed was an introduction to explain what had already been written. So I wrote a lengthy first half of the book to account for the thinking underpinning the already written second half. And the prologue to the whole thing was a little chapter called "Heidegger's Teacup." The book is about television (it is called *Television and the Meaning of "Live"*), but I needed to set out Heidegger's thinking first, because it underpinned everything I wanted to say about TV. And as he got older, Heidegger liked watching football on television.

Now, if you know him at all, you would know that Heidegger disapproved of television. His life spanned most of the twentieth century. He was born in Messkirch in 1889 (the same year, incidentally, that Wittgenstein was born) and died in 1976. Messkirch, at the time of Heidegger's birth, was a village with a population of around 2,000, situated in southwest Germany, just north of Lake Constance and the Swiss border. He grew up in a deeply rural, traditional Catholic environment; his father was a craftsman, a master cooper, and the sexton of the parish church. His mother's family were small tenant farmers. In 1961, Messkirch celebrated the 700th anniversary of its founding and it invited its most famous son, the now world-renowned philosopher, Martin Heidegger, to join in the festivities and give a talk. His talk, appropriately enough, was on the meaning of "home" and, he remarked, coming home to Messkirch today, the first thing one noticed was the forest of aerials on every rooftop. He saw in this a potent symbol of what the future held in store for Messkirch and the world. They showed that human beings were, strictly speaking, no longer "at home" where, seen from outside, they lived. The people of Messkirch might be sitting in their living-rooms, but really, thanks to television, they were in the sports stadium or on a safari or being a bystander at a gunfight in the OK Corral (see Pattison 2000: 59–60). The 71-year-old Heidegger was deeply suspicious of the intrusive, alien presence of television in people's homes. It was part of the domination of humankind by modern technology.

Heidegger, for sure, did not have a television set in his house. And yet, in his later years, he would regularly go to a friend's house to watch TV. All his life, he had been a keen sportsman. He was an excellent skier and would head for the snow-covered slopes whenever he could. He had always been fond of football and in his youth he was, as his biographer, Rudi Safranski tells us, a useful performer on the left wing. In later years he became an enthusiastic follower of the European Cup, watching it on television; "during one legendary match between Hamburg and Barcelona, he knocked over a teacup in his excitement" (Safranski 1998: 428). This match took place in the 1960–1 season, the same year in which Heidegger gave his talk in Messkirch.[4] Any good story has a moral to it, and this one raises the obvious question – if Heidegger disapproved so much of modern technology, why on earth did he get so excited watching a soccer match on the telly?

The point of this story is not what it meant in the book I wrote in 2014. An underlying motif in the chapter before this one is that in the *Lecture on Ethics*, there were two Wittgensteins in conflict with each other: the academic philosopher and the human being. And that points to the underlying theme of this one: Heidegger the famous academic philosopher, on the one hand, and, on the other, the ordinary human being who liked watching football on television. However, there is a big difference. As I read Wittgenstein's lecture I

---

[4] When exactly, during the game, Heidegger knocked over his teacup is (like the songs of the Sirens) beyond conjecture, but it was by all accounts a gripping, memorable match. Hamburg, the home team, was not well known outside Germany, while Barcelona was beginning to be mentioned in the same breath as Real Madrid, its historic rival and, at that time, the uniquely dominant club team in European football (Real had won the cup five times in succession at that point – every year, in fact, since the European Cup began in 1955). In the semifinal of the 1960–1 season, Hamburg, dominating throughout the match, was leading 2–1 when Barcelona scored in the last minute or so to force a replay. Barcelona won the replay and went into the final (having earlier knocked out Real Madrid) to be beaten, 3–2, by the leading Portuguese team, Benfica. All details from www.europeancuphistory.com.

felt that "the usual human being" and "the famous philosopher" were intrinsically entangled in it, and more generally throughout his life. I don't think that much of the philosophy, but I am deeply fascinated by Wittgenstein the man (and this is a pretty usual view). With Heidegger it is the reverse. I am blown away by the book that made him famous, but I'm not interested in his life, and I don't think all that much of him as a human being.

I

I had thought for a long time, before I read Heidegger, that television, and more generally broadcasting, was an ordinary, everyday thing. I was much impressed in my younger days, and still am, by the new post-war American sociology of Erving Goffman, Harold Garfinkel, and Harvey Sacks, and its turn to the careful study of ordinary, everyday life. I was deeply into their work well before I read Heidegger, and what I discovered was a kind of sociological phenomenology with its roots in Alfred Schutz. I mention this because what I call phenomenology is not just an academic, philosophical thing, and I am not just a fan of Heidegger. Nevertheless, the start-point for phenomenology (and it is an attitude, a disposition, not a theory) is the question of *experience*. And it began with two philosophers, Edmund Husserl and Martin Heidegger (who, to begin with, worked with the older Husserl). In his first publication, *Being and Time*, which came out in 1927, Heidegger transformed Husserlian phenomenology. I read it, not because I knew of or was interested in Heidegger and his thinking, but because a colleague, who knew I was interested in "ordinary life," said to me that I should read the work; thankfully, I did.

So what is his great work, *Being and Time*, about? It would be uncontentious to say that it is about the everyday world, and ordinary existence. Its *non-dit*, or given, is that the world he is writing about is the *human* world. And that means, as Heidegger puts it, *no ontotheology*. God is rigorously excluded from the analysis. Heidegger was brought up as a devout Catholic (he trained for the priesthood), but by the time he became an academic he had had a crisis of faith and no longer believed in organized religion (like Wittgenstein). The analysis of "being-in-the-world" in *Being and Time* (Dreyfus 1992) is discussed in relation to *Dasein*, Heidegger's word for "the usual human being." There was not a word in vernacular German for what Heidegger was after – a neutral term for "the ontology of being human." He wanted a word without biological, sociological, or psychological resonances. He was writing a text on one of the oldest, hoariest philosophical questions, which had long since fallen into intellectual desuetude. Ontology, or the question of being, went back to Plato (*Being and Time* starts with a quote from him) and became a mix of philosophy and theology as universities spread throughout Christian Europe from the thirteenth century onward. Indeed, because ontology, a key topic in medieval academic thinking, came to focus more and more on the existence (the Being) of God, Heidegger bent over backward to keep Him out of *Being and Time*. *His* topic was not the ontology of God, but of the human world. It was the world of *Dasein*, his catchword for ordinary life and ordinary human beings. The world, more exactly, was *Umwelt* – ordinary German word for which there no English equivalent unfortunately. It is usually translated as "the environment," which simply fails to capture the meaning-significance of *um*. The prefix means about, or surrounding – the roundabout-me world of everyday existence in which "I" or anyone am. The "I" here means the usual human being (sexed identity is irrelevant), completely immersed in the world as s/he encounters it. These two – the usual human world and the usual human beings who are immersed in it – are the interlocking themes of *Being and Time*.

The book was published in 1927 and consisted of two parts, Divisions One and Two. Heidegger's motive (his own personal reason) for writing *Being and Time* was that he needed a permanent academic job. He had published nothing, and to get tenure, as it's called in the USA, he needed to have published something, especially since his university wanted to offer him a named professorship (he had a tremendous reputation among the undergraduate population. He was known as "the hidden king of thought").[5] In the German educational system, academic tenure and promotion were not internal to the university. It depended on government approval. Heidegger at first wrote only Division One, which was submitted to the Board of Education as proof of his suitability for tenure as a full professor. Word came down the line that this, by itself, was not enough. So Heidegger went back to his lecture notes and hastily wrote up the next part (Division Two), to be

[5] The phrase itself was Hannah Arendt's description of her teacher, while she was an undergraduate at Freiburg (and Heidegger's secret lover). It draws upon a widespread folkloric myth of "the king who was asleep under the mountain." In Germany, it was associated with the twelfth-century Holy Roman Emperor, Frederick Barbarossa.

followed by the culminating third part (Division Three, never written) to be called "Time and Being," reversing the original title (Braver 2015). But One and Two were enough, and Heidegger got his professorship. And when both were printed together as *Being and Time*, it caused a sensation.

The full three-part book was never completed, and the published version has been described as a magnificent torso. Division One certainly stands alone on its own two feet, as a magnificent thing in itself. Its big idea is the question of *care* – in short, the care structure. Care is not some inner mentalistic state of mind ("the cares of the world," the burden of care, which is much the same as anxiety). It is not part of the psychology (the inner mental life) of the usual human. It is perhaps best thought of as what we now call infrastructure. This is a buzzword today, but it is not a new word for a new thing.

The final chapter of Division One is called "Care as the Being of *Dasein*" (1962: 225–311). Beneath the subsection title, "The Question of the Primordial Totality of Dasein's Structural Whole," it begins as follows: "Being-in-the-world is a structure which is primordially and constantly *whole*" (1962: 225). The human world is not one thing, and the usual human another. Being-in-the-world means *both, as inseparably interconnected*. It is not that there is a usual human who introjects the cares of the world, nor is it the other way about. A human world, in which anyone *is*, is necessarily made by human beings (this world, I have suggested, coming out of the "primordial" technology of writing). The historical world of everyday existence is, in all its parts and as a whole, a relational totality of material things, a techno-infrastructure. As such it cannot be separated from human beings who are its makers. The imbrication of each in the other amounts to a "relational totality of involvements," or, in other words, the "infrastructure."

This word itself, though it has come to the fore today as a technological term that goes with digitization, algorithms, and new media, goes back a couple of hundred years and in common usage once meant military, or environmental ensembles of things. But in Heidegger's thinking, the human world *and* those of us who live in it (we, the living) comprise the relational totality, the structure of care: the endless interplay between the world of usual things and the usual human beings who endlessly made, and make, and live in it.

II

It was the discovery of *this* world that so excited the young Heidegger. "Living in an environment [the standard English translation of *Umwelt*] signifies to me always and everywhere, it has all the character of world. *Es weltet* [It worlds]," he told his class in a lecture from 1919 (Figal 2009: 35). He had found a new way of "seeing" the world, which he called "the hermeneutics of facticity" – the interpretation of the ordinary world, as a matter of fact, and in a matter-of-fact way. This was the topic of a lecture course he gave to his undergraduate students at Freiburg in the summer semester of 1923. It was called, simply, "Ontology." But Heidegger starts off by claiming that traditional ontology (the philosophical *logos* or discourse, of *ontos* or being) can no longer get to grips with its question – the meaning of *ontos*. A new approach was needed that depended on the careful analysis of mundane life, because this was all we knew. It was what we were immersed in: the humanly made (the historical) world.

Toward the end of the course Heidegger discusses two different ways in which we encounter everyday things – a table, say – in the usual world:

> In *the* room there at home stands *the* table (not "a" table among many other tables in other rooms and houses) at which one sits *in order to* write, have a meal, sew, play . . . Its standing-there in the room means: Playing this role in such and such characteristic use. This or that is "impractical," unsuitable. That part is damaged. It now stands in a better spot in the room than before – there's better lighting for example. Where it stood before was not at all good (for . . .). Here and there it shows lines – the boys like to busy themselves at the table. These lines are not just interruptions in the paint, but rather [it means]: it was the boys and still is. This side is not the east side, and this narrow side so many cm. shorter than the other, but rather this is the side at which my wife sits in the evening when she wants to stay up and read; there at the table we had such and such a discussion; there that decision was made with a *friend*; there that *work* written that time; there that *holiday* celebrated that time. (1999 [1923]: 69)

A table, any table, a table Thing. Any table (as a universal) can be *objectively* described and defined in terms of its objective observable and determinable properties. It (any table) is made of such and such materials. It stands so high. It is x centimeters long and y centimeters wide and it weighs so much etc. On the other hand, *the* table (*this* table) is a particular thing, a taken-for-granted given in my family's life. Heidegger clarifies the significance of the table (what it *means* to him, as distinct from what objectively it *is*) as part of a world for those for whom it matters. Its significance lies in the ways that it matters. It is significant because it is put to significant use. *This* is what we do at the table, Heidegger says: I write; my wife reads or sews; my young sons play and (literally) leave their mark upon it. They have scored its surface with their pencils so that, whenever he sees those marks, Heidegger is reminded of their presence. The table is marked with their being. They have impressed themselves upon it in their own small way. Such are the everyday structures of significance in and for which the table is a part.

Everyday things are everywhere imbued with the presence of particular some ones. Any thing can be transformed to appear as some thing: a transformation brought about by someone impressing upon the thing the mark of their being. You can tell that a living-room bears the mark of the people who live in it. You see this without noticing it really in the things that show as theirs – mementoes, keepsakes, ornaments, and souvenirs – in all the bric-a-brac, the seen but unnoticed clutter in the room. A room stripped of such stuff is not a homely (lived-in) room. Some years ago, I stood in the empty living-room of the house in which my mother had lived for so many years; the house in which I and my brothers and sisters grew up, and from which she had moved because now, in old age, it was too difficult living there alone. Stripped of all its familiar things – these photo-graphs of the family on the mantelpiece, that set of china in the corner cupboard (a wedding present), the three-piece suite of furniture chosen after much deliberation – the room (the house itself) no longer bore the marks of her presence. The house, which *was* her life, *upon which* she had impressed her being there, was no more so. Her being that once was there was now gone and would not return. Places stripped of the presence of particular someones may have an aesthetic purity. They may be technically efficient. But they are strictly impersonal, as are so many public, institutional rooms – lecture and seminar rooms for instance.

Heidegger goes on to imagine the "awhileness" of the table in his living room:

> That is *the* table – as such it is there in the temporality of everydayness, and as such will it perhaps be encountered again after many years when, having been taken apart and now unusable, it is found lying on the floor somewhere, just like other "things," e.g. a plaything, worn out and almost unrecognizable – it is my youth. In a corner of the basement stands an old pair of skis, one of which is broken in half – what stands there are not material things of different lengths, but rather the skis from that time, from that adventure with so and so. . . . These are characteristics of the world's being encountered. What now needs to be enquired into is how *they constitute the being-there of the world*. (1999 [1923]: 69–70; translation slightly modified and final emphasis added)

The table ("now") and the old pair of skis ("then") are part of Heidegger's youth. It is not just we ourselves, but our things too (the things we care for) that change *in* time. In our living room, in a basket covered over by a jumble of other things, is a small stuffed pony made of wool. This is – or, rather, was – Nitty; Princess Nitty Noy of Noyland, in the make-believe world created by my daughter when she was a little girl. This world once was for her (and for me) real, true, and alive. It is so no longer because my now grown-up daughter has long since grown out of the games of her childhood. But it is hard to imagine throwing Nitty away even though she no longer has any "use." This small thing is full of memories. In it, I still see (I still hear) the traces of my daughter as she once was, when she was five or six. Nitty still brings flooding back a time in our life together that has gone for us both and yet which somehow (in our hearts) is carried forward in the present.

This is something of the significance of everyday things as taken for granted aspects of our lives. Does that mean they are just "personal" and "subjective"? Is not Nitty "in fact" just a mass-produced consumer good for kids onto which one particular child has projected her own particular childish fantasies? Maybe. But is it not rather that my daughter put the thing (the toy) to use in an appropriate way? Any toy has "to-be-played-with" as its "for-the-sake-of-which," and this is inscribed in its design, in the materials from which it is made, its shape and size and so on. Just as the table elicits a wide range of involvements – eating, sewing, reading, playing, talking – and is "for" these things, so too a small woollen toy elicits a range of behaviors that are appropriate to it and my daughter found one. She discovered (invented) an appropriate thing to do with it. She "created" Nitty. She brought her into being. For a while at least, Nitty was not an imaginary projection onto what was "in fact" just stuff (material, physical matter) put together in a particular way. Nitty was real and alive for my daughter and for me. She was, for a while, part of our family life. A toy "is" a meaning structure, the relational totality of involvements that the toy elicits. To this care structure my young daughter brought herself and her concerns (*her* care structure) and impressed them both upon the toy in her own small and unique way. The interaction between humans and humanly made thing is the infrastructure.

What intersected in the play of the game (the created world of Noyland) was the impersonal care structure of a mass-produced thing and the personal care and concern that my daughter brought to it. It would be wholly wrong, though, to imagine that the former is the actual and objective "reality," while the latter is "just" a subjective, imaginary projection upon it. My daughter did indeed project herself upon the woollen toy. But her particular "upon which" (*her* game) was, in a general sense, anticipated and allowed for, in the toy's design and manufacture, as an appropriate appropriation of it. Everyday things have a "they" structure (they are for anyone), but upon such structures we impress ourselves and, in so doing, transform them and make them part of our lives. As such they accompany us through life and are the placeholders of meaningful events, places, moments, and relationships in the course of a lifetime. *This* was given me by my wife at the beginning of our relationship before we married. *That* I bought on a particular journey abroad. When I listen to *this* song, I remember a particular time, a place, a person. These are the structures of significance in which we dwell for a while in the round-about-me world of everydayness.

III

I was dumbfounded by this. It seemed to me to be both true and beautiful, and I felt myself forever in Heidegger's debt (and still do) for helping me to see things in this way.

I saw the world afresh, and as if for the first time (like my little daughter). I saw it through Heidegger's eyes, as he patiently worked his way through to the end of Division One. Everything was different, and yet the same. In the book I wrote about television I wanted to show something of the hidden workings or care structures of both the production process itself and all that we listen to and watch. I made careful studies of two old programs; one from British radio during World War Two, one from American television of 1953. I wanted to show how they worked, in order to make visible something of the hidden labor that went into their production, the concealed given of their infrastructure. So I wrote a chapter called "How to Talk – on Television," which followed on from a chapter called "How to Talk – on Radio." Talk, as we've seen, is as old as humankind. But it only became *historical* when radio and then television broadcasting came along. And that depended on when radio and then television made talk a matter of record. I think of both as technologies of talk. Not *just* that, naturally, but radio for sure, and I think of television as the same as radio, with vision added on (it used to be known as "talking heads"). Although both are different media with similar and different affordances, the content of both is the same. The "contents" of radio (its spread of program genres) were taken over and rethought for television. There is no program genre peculiar to television that cannot be found on radio (I can't think of one at least), though there are significant differences of emphasis (there's a lot more music on radio than there is on television). But all depend on the care structures of talk, and writing.

One of the problems of talk on early radio was that it was all scripted, and sounded as though it was just that.

It was boring. It lacked the immediacy and spontaneity of usual (unscripted) talk between people in everyday life. The first completely unscripted formatted "talk show" in the UK (not how it was thought of at the time) was *The Brains Trust*, a wartime "entertainment show" that consisted of a "host" and four panel members, answering ad lib – and not knowing them in advance – questions sent in by members of the listening public. The studio panel consisted of the usual suspects, public men who were used to public speaking (Scannell 2014: 107–18). They were not, though, speaking from a script and their spontaneous responses made the program a sensation. The show's format was copied in village and church halls up and down the land. What everyone loved was the sound of talk-as-discussion itself, real, authentic, unscripted, *live*.

In the early years of television in the UK, the BBC started newscasting only because commercial television was imminent, and part of the whole new challenge to public service broadcasting was ITN, Independent Television News, whose job was to provide a daily national news service for the network of commercial TV stations all over the British Isles. To get ahead of the curve, the BBC went ahead with its own television news service in the run-up to the start of ITV. And it was a disaster, much mocked by the national press. It was, in effect, a radio bulletin read by an unseen voice over a sequence of still photographs, occasional silent filmed news clips, maps, diagrams, and captions. There was a hasty internal review, and it was quickly conceded that it was necessary to have a newsreader in the studio to present the news, provide continuity between items, and hold it all together.

Senior radio newsreaders were co-opted, but they confronted an immediate difficulty: how *do* you read the news to camera? This was not a problem for radio, but it was for television. If the newsreader just keeps his eyes on the script all the time, it makes for a visibly peculiar viewing experience. Is he reading aloud to himself? Why doesn't he look at me? So newsreaders were asked to look at the camera as much as they could, but this was equally disconcerting. With eyes that constantly flickered up and down from the script on the desk to the camera in front of them, newsreaders (all male in those far off times) came across as positively shifty and furtive – as if they could not bring themselves to look the honest viewer in the eye. And they were prone to lose their place in the script as their eyes moved continually away from and back to it. The *Daily Mirror* (a leading British tabloid) ran a two-page spread with the banner headline "THESE ARE THE GUILTY MEN" and beneath it photographs of BBC newsreaders with eyes downcast on the script or looking (seemingly nervously) up from it.

As we all know, the solution to this problem was the auto-cue, or teleprompter, a technical device developed in the USA in the early 1950s, and immediately taken up in Britain and elsewhere, precisely to secure the "sincerity effect" of direct eye contact with each and every viewer. This "look-to-camera" is peculiar to television (it is never used in classic cinema, because it disrupts the fictionality of film narrative that depends on the willing suspension of disbelief). It generates a standard Gricean implicature: "I am being spoken to." It implicates a real-world interaction between the speaker in the studio (not an actor) and any individual real-world viewer (in each case "me") at home or wherever. And this contributes to the taken-for-granted effect that television news is a fact, not a fiction. The invention of the teleprompter was one small but significant contribution to produce this overall effect.

IV

Today, news-talk is the one broadcast television genre that still relies on the written word as its bedrock, writing as the guarantor of its truth.[6] Leaving aside fictional drama, which depends on actors who have learned their lines, just about everything else is unscripted talk. But this is a learned behavior, and we, who are used to it, expect it. What also needed to be learned, for the first time, on early television as much as on radio, was unscripted talk, not a speech written down and read aloud like Wittgenstein's talk on ethics to the Heretics. A very early step in this direction was a CBS program that began in the fall of 1953 called *Person to Person*, hosted by Ed Murrow. The program's big idea was to build it around unscripted talk. The guests (they were all very well-known Americans) were invited to do two things: show viewers a bit of their home and sit down for a little informal talking. "Who knows," Murrow said in his invitation to them, "in spite of television, it may still be possible to revive the art of conversation."

The problem was, though, that Murrow was conversationally challenged. He was a household name as

---

[6] Until today. "Fake news" is an effect of new tele-technologies that have undermined the unquestionable authority of writing over speech as the record of truth upon which printed and broadcast news depend.

a journalist/interviewer on wartime radio and subsequently early television. But when it came to ordinary unscripted talk in a person-to-person interaction (like the SFE), he was hopelessly wooden, particularly with glamorous women. His much anticipated "conversation" with Marilyn Monroe was toe-curlingly awful. "Does she make her own bed?" he asked her friend (with whom she was staying in upstate New York). "Have you ever been to the circus?" he asked Monroe herself. The very early show that I studied was broadcast and recorded live to air in October 1953. Murrow was to meet with the young Senator, John F. Kennedy, and his newly married wife, Jacqueline Bouvier, in the Senator's Boston apartment.

I was interested in all the ways in which the little program (it ran for just under fifteen minutes) was *not* what we'd call "good television." It came across as labored and staged. The brief tour of the Kennedy apartment had a leaden predictability about it, with conversational props all too clearly flagged up as just that. And Murrow's conversation with Mrs. Kennedy was, like his conversation with Marilyn Monroe, a disaster. Talk is a live two-way interaction and the aim of the series was to make it into a new form of public entertainment. But it took years for this to be an achieved and accomplished fact of broadcast television. The various ways in which the meeting with the Kennedys went wrong showed, by a perspective of incongruity, what we all take for granted in broadcasting: that the experience of watching television *is* precisely that (an experience), because it is, apparently, effortlessly produced. If the program does not work, for whatever reason, it will seem labored and staged, not a relaxed (an *accomplished*) thing. The awkwardnesses of *Person to Person* made visible the hidden labor of its making. It troubles our expectation that things will work easily and effortlessly. It is this huge, all-pervasive, natural, and taken-for-granted trust in them that underpins our everyday world and conversations. And this is the overall effect of the broadcast production care structures that we neither hear nor see.[7]

V

As a thought experiment of the kind Wittgenstein was fond of, or even as a joke, think about how many television cameras you'd need to cover a football match. One will do, surely. Maybe two. All you need do is to position a camera at a convenient height on the halfway line, and you have end-to-end coverage. But, routinely, at least twenty or more cameras are set in place ahead of the game for big matches. Why so many, if one or two will do? We might remember the words of Bill Shankly, the famed Liverpool manager, who once remarked that football was not a matter of life and death. "It's much more serious than that." Soccer *is* a serious matter, and a big soccer match is a great occasion. Television coverage must reflect this. Even the most exciting matches have longish periods in which not a lot is happening, and for most of the time routine coverage is indeed produced by what Ed Buscombe (1975) calls "the prime camera," positioned at the halfway line, roughly at the

---

[7] My interpretation of *Person to Person* is not a personal, retrospective thing (being wise after the event), but is based on the frame-by-frame analysis of the visuals, and an analysis of the verbatim transcription of the talk. It also draws upon contemporary responses to the series, which were overwhelmingly unfavourable along the lines that I indicate (2014: 128–39).

same height as the commentary boxes for the sports journalists.

But when a goal is scored, all this changes. Goals, when they come, do not follow a script. They are expected, of course, but are still utterly unpredictable. They come and go in a flash. When a goal hits the net, an immediate, visual narrative routine kicks in, quite different from routine coverage of the game. In quick succession, a number of different cameras from various vantage points around the ground offer shots that are woven, by a special "goals unit," into a sequence that, with slight variations, is always the same. From the moment the ball is in the net, the narrative runs as follows: shot of the goal scorer; shot of the team manager; shot of the fans whooping in delight; shot of other members of the team piling on top of the goal scorer; instant replay 1 of the goal; instant replay 2 from a different angle; instant replay 3 from another angle; back to the prime camera and routine coverage of the game.

This sequence is a format, a formula that follows routinely, automatically, whenever a goal is scored. But notice how it works: it follows the Gricean communicative logic of implicatures. The sequence is a series of rapid cuts, from one shot to another. Cutting, in film and television, presupposes that the viewer will figure out what links shot b to a, c to b and so on. The first pair of shots (a > b) is what conversation analysis would call "canonical." The prime camera shows the goal going into the net, after which there is always an immediate cut to a close-up of an individual player who is, one way or another, obviously delighted. Who could this be? The answer is obviously the person who scored the goal, although this is not said. It is simply a standard implicature that anyone can understand: after the ball is in the net, the next most relevant thing to show (the maxim of relation) is the person who scored the goal. And the logic of the sequence (it is simply not any old thing, one after another; and the baby's effort to reconnect with her mother has the same temporal narrative logic) is a continuing display, in order of relevance, of those most immediately affected by the goal – the goal scorer, the team manager, and the team players. There is some variation in the sequence overall, but not in the canonical what-next shot of the goal scorer. The maxim of relevancy, that accounts for all the shots (the inner logic of the sequence), depends on temporal adjacency. Each shot in turn is the next most relevant thing to follow the immediately preceding shot. And nobody was ever told how to decode what happens on television when a goal is scored. We all just figure it out, if we notice it at all. What we see, what we get to experience in a unique way, is the goal itself, its impact and effect. We do not see the hidden technical production skills that "give" us the experience of it. And yet it requires a high degree of concerted professional competence to produce the sequence time and time again, and always perfectly.

Does soccer coverage *need* the deployment of two dozen cameras to produce the game as something to be watched by absent viewers? Of course not. The overhead blimp shot, from a stationary airship moored high above the stadium, deployed in big matches, is quite pointless and unnecessary, so why is it there? It is there because television does indeed work to inflate the occasion, to make something of it, to enhance its mood. It is but one tiny instance of what Frances Bonner so beautifully calls television's transformative "gift of attention"

– its focused attentiveness to the task of doing "being there" as best it can for and on behalf of every viewer (2003: 127). The overhead blimp shot (like the icing on a cake) is either a pointless waste of money, or else it is one seen, but unnoticed, way in which the significance of a big occasion is unobtrusively underscored in the way that television covers it. Whether you prefer a deflationary or an inflationary interpretation of this particular shot does not negate the opposing view that you reject. Both are true.

If the blimp shot is unnecessary, the narrative format that clicks in automatically when goals are scored is perhaps even more superfluous to requirements. It is indeed inflationary. And yet it is truly wonderful; an extraordinary, unobtrusive display of the capacity of broadcast television both to *be* in the moment while simultaneously recording it, and instantly retrieving the moment just now gone in replays from different angles whenever goals are scored. It is essentially awesome and mysterious, when you come to think of it. Only the tele-technologies of radio and television could produce the magical replay shots, bringing the moment just past into the present moment once more, thereby creating an "impossible" doubled temporality: the present moment, and the moment just now gone, in the same-time-now. What *is* the point of this little narrative that kicks in when a goal is scored? Is it part of TV hype? I do not think so. That is to say that I do not think that the audiovisual narrative format that I have analyzed is something externally superimposed on the moment of the goal in order, as it were, to make more of it than it merits. Rather, it seems to me to be an uncalled-for gift that is true to the inner meaning of "the moment," working to realize its authenticity. And all this hidden labor, this care and attentiveness, explains why, perhaps, Heidegger got so involved in the soccer match he was watching, that he knocked over his cup of tea in excitement.

5
Miracles

The live coverage of a soccer game (in American football, it's three or four hours) is "lived time," the time of the politics of the present. And the moment of the goal that comes and goes in an eyeblink (an *Augenblick*) is an instant, immediate, ecstatic temporality. Both are aspects of the temporal politics of the present. Yet Heidegger's book is called *Being* – and *Time*, and time is a long time arriving. The whole of Division One of the book (which is nearly three hundred pages long) is about the spatiality of the human world. Division Two, which is about "fallenness" and time, has received far less attention. Hubert Dreyfus, who wrote *Being-in-the-World*, a widely read textbook that put *Being and Time* on the map in the United States, simply ignores Division Two completely as being less intelligible than Division One.

It is true that Division Two reads more like the author talking to himself than to the reader, as Heidegger tries to figure out the hermeneutics of time. But human temporality was on his mind in the 1920s, and in 1924 he gave a talk, subsequently published as *The Concept*

of Time, to the theological faculty at Freiburg (1992
[1924]). He began with the theological order of time that
is known as eternity. But this, he tactfully points out, is
God's time and belongs to theology. He is a philosopher
and his start point is human, not divine, being. His overall theme is time and everydayness compared with the
time of nature and the time of the world (1992 [1924]:
3E). From this, and other writings subsequently published, a reasonably clear picture can be pieced together
of how Heidegger conceived of time. But it remained
unclear in Division Two, and the projected third part,
"Time and Being," never appeared (Braver 2015). But
what is clear, as its title suggests, and this is borne out
in Division Two, is that *time was the horizon of being*.
All things are in time. But what I think he meant is that
all *living* things (including us) are in time. And for that
matter, I think the motif of "being-in-the-world" should
more exactly be understood as "being (alive and living)
in the (shared) world (with others)." Be that as it may,
Heidegger's musings on time are all based on the existential temporality of individual human lifetime. But
that begs the question of historical time. The time of
history, of *longue durée*, stretches over countless generations. Quite unlike the finitude of individual lifetime,
sociological time (the times of human societies, as distinct from the time of the world) stretches out before us
into an indefinite future.

As a child, I wondered what it would be like to be
grown up. That was then before me, the unknown
future. There was nothing behind me. I had no past. And
I duly did become, in time, an adult, going to university,
getting a job, getting married, having children, getting
divorced. And the upshot of all this was that I became,

in various ways, experienced in a general way as I accumulated a past. They go together – time and experience. This stretch lasted quite a long time, fifty years of teaching in fact. And then I stopped work, and now I'm writing this. For Heidegger, being-toward-the-future meant the acceptance of mortality, and I agree with him (though he forgets the messianic promise of natality, and that birth and death presuppose each other). But all the while, through the course of my life, I have faced the future in the present, like any usual human being.

I

There are many orders of time, but two basic ones are analogue and digital temporalities. The former is very old, the latter very new. Digital time became a temporal reality with the introduction, in the 1970s, of digital watches on the mass market. Hitherto, clocks and watches represented what retronymically came to be thought of as *analogue* time, the time of the analogue watch (the first patent on a digital clock was taken out in the USA in the 1950s). Then, timepieces were called simply clocks or watches because everybody took their time from them. But, just as the VCR was a seventies thing, so too was a digital watch. Both "tell" the time, more exactly, the punctual *now!* But the analogue and digital timepiece do the same thing differently. Digital time is numbered. When I look at my digital watch it gives me the exact time now. Now it is 13:15, 13:16, 13:17 etc., etc. There is no reference to the temporalities of before and after. But when I look at my (analogue) watch, I say it's a quarter past one, or a quarter to one. Digital time has no sense of past or future. It is always, only, and ever, the time *now!* We are, I might say, caught forever in an endless present. But in the analogue system, time is in motion as it moves, like the hands of the clock or watch, from the past into the future. Analogue time is cyclical, digital time is linear.

Exact time measurement is a contemporary preoccupation, as the human relationship with time has changed over the centuries. In the past, people wanted to know the time of day or the season of the year. They needed to know the time in order to do the right thing (a time to sow, a time to reap, a time for everything). Watches only became something that everyone had in the twentieth century, as the mechanisms themselves (through continuing economic/technical innovation) became smaller, more mobile, and cheaper. Today, we live in a 24/7 world, and everything has speeded up – there is no longer time for everything – a time to get the kids to school, time for the meeting, the lesson, and so on – an endless rush.

Historical time, which is made in the temporality of the present by the generations of the living, has two axes. In any present now there is, for any one, the present><future and the present><past stretched out on the elastic timeline of life. Lifetime is existentially linear as I or any historical person experiences it. It implacably has a beginning, an in-between (the present, the time of the living), and an end. But the time of history is not just lifetime stretched out further. It is a different order of time altogether. Lifetime is radically definite (the one thing we all know is that it *will* end in my case). Historical time is radically indefinite, stretching far back into the remote past, and forward into the immeasurable future. It has been, until the last century, wholly

dependent on writing until radio and television came along and introduced new orders of historicality – time according to radio, time according to television.

As an historical person, I live in both temporal orders: the time of the life that is mine, and the time of human history. These two different orders of existential time now mesh well together so that the time of history smooths over the ruin of individual human lifetime and death. In the past, to take English history as an instance, the death of the monarch was always a crisis, provoking other powerful families to contest the succession and fight for the crown. It has taken many generations to set in place supervening temporal political and socio-cultural institutions that are adjusted to lifetime, while belonging to the surpassing order of historical or institutional time. It is not that history is relative; rather, we, the living, are relative to the time of history, which is an order of time that reaches far beyond any individual lifetime, looking both back and forward.

Historical time, the time of history, is brought into being by writing. It stands in relation to two other orders of time: the time of the world, and the time of the universe. Historical time belongs to human beings. The time of the world belongs to God. But to whom does the time of the universe belong? I haven't the foggiest idea. And I don't care. I leave it to the scientists to bicker among themselves about it. The universe is *very* ancient. It exists in infinite time–space. And the big bang happened billions of years ago. I don't know how many exactly, but, at any rate, time began (and also space) at some point (big bang theory). Scientists get very excited by the first nanoseconds of time when the universe (or universes) got going. And time here means scientific time, and all that means is that time (in scientific thought) is numbered, and numbers mean writing.

Time for me is, like language, an effect of writing. Prehistorical time appears to presuppose that it comes before history, the *prehistorical* age. But that notion – of time before history – imagines time as always already given in advance. But only for us, I think – historical humans who live in time. Indeed, I simply cannot think outside time, which I naturally understand in terms of past, present, and future; beginnings, middles, and endings. Human time is historical time, and from this I get my notion of death.[8] To think of it in this way is to make time humanly intelligible. Unintelligible time – time we just cannot imagine – belongs to God and His world. Simply by growing up and thus becoming highly literate through a lengthy formal education, I have grown out of God's world and time, like Tara Westover. As far as I can tell, being alive and living in the human world does depend on time. And my human sense of time depends on unimagining it as a precondition for entry into God's world once more. And I just can't do that.[9]

---

[8] Only historical humans know that they will die. Of course, all living things, as we would say, die, but that does not presuppose that they know this. At some point they just stop living but, unlike you and me, they just *are*, whereas as we *are* and *know* that we are (and that includes knowing that we shall die).

[9] The highly compressed argument of this section supposes that time is a purely human invention that, like history and language, becomes available through writing. Heidegger never clarifies what, in fact, *being* means. But evidently *Being and Time* is about the human world and no other. It only takes a few twiddles of the dial to see that time (our uniquely human sense of temporality in terms of past–present–future) is the infrastructure of the living world (divine and human). This is the big idea, for me, of Division One of *Being and Time*. Heidegger thought of it as the care structure – the endless interplay of human beings and everyday technology (tables, for instance, or skis). Later he would fret over modern technologies (but he liked

II

The author of the *Tractatus* could only conceive of the objective worlds of fact: the world as everything that is the case. What is the case is a fact. Science recognizes this and is concerned solely with the world of empirically verifiable facts. Fact-things (objects in object-worlds) can be known objectively in terms of empirically determined facts about them based on (a) a careful human observation of their observable properties, and (b) careful measurement of them – length, breadth, and depth, for instance, which establish the three spatial dimensions of observable things. The *Tractatus* set out the chilly logic of the knowable world of things, and science is concerned with knowledge (epistemology, to give it its philosophical name). Wittgenstein claimed there was nothing more to be said after his book, and philosophy was now finished. But part of his restless genius was to see through the ideas of the *Tractatus*.

In his *Lecture on Ethics*, Wittgenstein saw that science had nothing to say about miracles. It was a different way of saying what the *Tractatus* left unsaid – everything in that text was about the knowable world of (scientific, aka logical) facts. What it meant, however, according to its author, was its ethical *non-dit*, everything it did not say. Miracles (like unicorns) are not facts. It is not that Wittgenstein believed in miracles. He just knew that some things (life, for instance) were miraculous. This knowing was not based on the epistemology of science.

watching football on the telly) – fearing, I think, that we lived in an axial age of historical time in which human><machine interaction was being displaced by machine><human and machine><machine interactions.

It was quite different from that. And yet he wanted (he longed for) the certainty of scientific knowledge. In the last months of his life, he was preoccupied by G. E. Moore's common-sense arguments against the sceptic's objections to certainty (Wittgenstein 1969). And this contradiction – between the (academic) scientific world of facts, and the numinous world of miracles – ran through all his later thought and writings.

Wittgenstein's miracle was the wonder of the world, not the universe that scientifically minded folk go starry-eyed about. I have no ideas whatever about the universe. And God is not the lord of the universe. He is the Creator of this world, the one I live in. As a member of historical humanity, I do not count myself as one of God's creatures. I do though think that the world is one thing, and the universe (which belongs to science) is something else. When I say or think, as I sometimes do, that when God's in His heaven all's right with the world, I do mean this world, planet Earth, on which I dwell with several billion other human beings, some of whom believe in God and are members of faith communities. I've always thought of Him as the Lord of life, and life as belonging to this particular planet whose uniqueness (which I took for granted) is now very much in question. Science has discovered a load of exo-planets all over the universe, and what does that say about God and the lonely uniqueness of planet Earth? Do they all have their own special God, like I had my angel as my mother told me? It is hard to avoid thinking of Him as an omni-scientist of some sort, as John Peters seems to think (2015: 315–87). But I am, like Wittgenstein, quite easy with bringing "God" into this narrative without any nostalgia for organized religion, although I have fond memories of being once a Catholic, for whom miracles were just facts of life, like angels.

III

One of the last things I did before I stopped teaching and returned home to England was to offer a final-year undergraduate course on animals and the media. I look back on it now, and I do not think it was much good. I made up the whole course myself – all readings and viewings – because there was no body of academic writing on this topic that I could appeal to. The course ran for fifteen weeks, and the effort of holding it all together nearly killed me. Nevertheless, I produced the appropriate number of written assignments, and all the students were properly graded in the end. So, *they* were satisfied. But for all its obvious weaknesses, I learned something important from the sheer labor of creating and working my way through the course. And that is why, I now see, I put it all together in the first place. My takeaway thought was the realization that we, human beings, no longer share the world with other nonhuman creatures. We simply take it as read that the world belongs to us, and only us. The course-book, the one we all read at the beginning, was Peter Singer's *Animal Liberation* (1995 [1975]), and what an eye-opener it was for me. The abuse of animals by the global agricultural industry is shocking and shameful. The mass manufacture of livestock – chickens, pigs, cows – I could hardly bear to read it. We had good classroom discussions about eating animal flesh and the ethics of vegetarianism. We made a special study of our nearest nonhuman relatives (gorillas and chimpanzees) in the movies – from *Bedtime for Bonzo*, starring Ronald Reagan and a chimpanzee, to *The Story of Nim*, a documentary movie about the life of a chimpanzee caught up in the scientific craze of the 1970s to teach our nearest animal neighbors how to communicate with us. The treatment of Nim himself by the scientists involved in the project was as mindlessly barbaric as the treatment of Genie Wiley at more or less the same time. From the course, I came to think of God not so much as omniscient, but as frail and vulnerable. I could no longer just take Him, and His world, and His creatures, as simple facts of life as I had done in my carefree childhood.

Nowadays, I occasionally think of God as a psychoanalyst (He behaves rather like Sigmund Freud). The patient on the couch is always the Present, who speaks for all who are alive and living in the world at the time. Generation after generation, the Present enters, lies down on the couch, and starts telling God of its experiences. And always it says the same thing: that it doesn't understand what's going on, and things aren't working out, and it doesn't know what to do. God is very, very bored with the way that history (which is made in and by the Present) endlessly repeats itself. His advice is always the same: life and history are lived going forward but understood backward (God has Kierkegaard, of whom He is rather fond, in mind). To understand life, you must reflect on your own experience of it. Only in the past does the Present ever begin to make sense.

IV

The God of the universe (if there is such a Being) is a proxy for scientific certainty. In his play *Back to Methuselah*, first performed in 1922, George Bernard Shaw imagined superintelligent beings of AD 31,920 growing out of the concerns of art, science, and sex ("these childish games – this dancing, and singing and mating") and turning away to think about mathematics (Hodges 2012: 161). As an undergraduate at Cambridge, Alan Turing sat in on some of the lectures in Wittgenstein's undergraduate course on the foundation of mathematics, which he gave in 1939 (Hodges 2012: 193–6; Monk 1991: 417–22). Turing is now regarded as the one person, more than any other, who created the world we now live in, which is totally dependent on what he called "thinking machines," or Turing machines, and which we now know as digital computers. Turing foresaw our fully technologized, digital world. Human-inspired "intelligence" was too emotional to be applied to his machines. He preferred to argue that they could think, not that they were intelligent. The two words were not interchangeable. The issue was discussed on the BBC's Third Programme,[10] with Turing arguing that he did not want to give a definition of thinking (Copeland 1994: 487–506). The important thing was to try and draw a line between the properties of a brain, or of a man. Instead of offering a definition of thinking, he proposed a test, the famous Turing Test. "The idea was that the machine has to try and pretend to be a man, by answering questions put to it, and it will only pass if

---

[10] The BBC's Third Programme was a national radio channel (1946–67) that supposedly addressed the interests of the educated, intellectual elite, such as Turing and co. Alas, not many people listened to it, including the minority elite it claimed to address. It was replaced by Radio Three, a dedicated classical music channel that addressed the same supposed audience's supposed musical tastes.

the pretence is reasonably convincing" (Copeland 2004: 495). The questioners were in one room, the machine in another, and its replies were sent back as typewritten answers. This, Turing admitted, was not the same as "Do machines think?," but it was near enough, and raised the same difficulties.

For Turing, thinking and reasoning were the same. Reasoning was a step-by-step process, one move at a time. It was logical. This process could be performed by a computing machine, although, in the 1930s, a computer normally meant a person making calculations. Turing's most famous paper was on computable numbers in relation to a human computer and a computing machine (Copeland 2004: 91–124). He was a mathematical logician and an engineer (like Wittgenstein). He was the father of Artificial Intelligence (AI) – though he disliked the notion of intelligence – and ultimately of robotics. A thinking machine needed memory so that it could build up experience; in other words, it could learn. The memory store allowed the machine itself to modify its behavior in interaction with other machines. And all this depended on the binary language of digital numbers (0 and 1) as the code in which human computers (nowadays, programmers) wrote the program (or algorithm) that defined the telos of the machine (what it could do, its aim or purpose). For Turing, an electronic machine was a living thing defined by its on/off switch, so that when you turned it on, it came to (artificial) life (Copeland 2004: 362–506). It was a clear implication of Turing's work that machines were like humans, because both had brains, but machines were not human. He did not imagine a world in which machines could reproduce themselves, and possibly have an existence that was completely independent of human life. This remains the stuff of science fiction and the movies, but Turing had created a robotic future as a real possibility.

This was very different from Wittgenstein's way of thinking. For sure, he was part of the emerging new order of thinking, based on the new theory of mathematics, laboriously elaborated by a distinguished body of mathematicians and philosophers, from the mid-nineteenth century onwards. The difference between Wittgenstein and Turing came down to whether or not they would ("theoretically") tolerate a contradiction. This became an irresolvable difference between them, which arose as Turing sat in on Wittgenstein's lectures (the lectures became, in effect, a discussion between the two of them). From a mathematical point of view, a system of logic, for it to be perfect, could have no internal contradictions, for that would allow for possible exceptions or mistakes. But for Wittgenstein, contradictions were a feature of ordinary language, and human life. A contradiction was a paradox, the exception that proves the rule. For Turing, science needed to be exactly right, completely so, and thus the possibility of system error (the bridge collapsing) required a fundamental theoretical rethink. Human beings could make mistakes, but not a Turing machine. Wittgenstein thought that this objection (if a mistake in calculation is made, maybe the bridge will fall down) was trivial, like the Liar's Paradox. Turing was far ahead of his own time, and received posthumous recognition only many years after his untimely death. He is now regarded as a model of scientific (mathematical) thinking, and when you let science in, "where has the miracle gone"?

I say, "It's a lovely day," and it's raining cats and

dogs outside. The weather contradicts what I've said. Am I stupid, or somehow misinformed (are all my senses working satisfactorily)? No, I'm just being ironic. It is a perfectly acceptable thing to *say*, and my saying so is just a way of making conversation, or being sociable. I am not, in fact, contradicting the external (rainy) world. What I say is only a contradiction in an abstract (literal) system of writing, and is, as such, intolerable. And this is the force of Grice's theory of communication: that is, of saying one thing, and meaning something else entirely. There is something doggedly straightforward in scientific thinking for which a contradiction is a catastrophe in any theory and must lead to its abandonment. And this, for me, explains how a miracle (any contradiction) can be acceptable (can exist in fact) only in a nonscientific world. Science cannot accept miracles. They have gone out of the window. Perhaps I am being unfair. Scientists do have a sense of wonder. But on closer inspection, their sense of wonder is a sense of awe at the vastness of the universe. Wittgenstein, you may remember, extended Moore's definition of ethics to include aesthetics. But he never got round to saying anything more about it. And a scientific sense of wonder is basically a numerical thing: the beauty of mathematics, unimaginably large numbers, and unimaginably small ones. But scientific wonder at the majesty of the universe is not the same as the miracle of the actually existing world. I might say, to contradict myself for a moment, that I'm certain the world exists, but not the universe. I care about the former, but not the latter. But then, I'm not a scientist.

Wittgenstein died of cancer, in a friend's house, just turned sixty-two. He was expecting to see some friends who were coming to pay their last respects. Shortly before he lapsed into unconsciousness, he said to Mrs. Bevan, who looked after him, "Tell them I had a wonderful life" – his "famous last words." In the end, it was life, rather than language, that was a thing of wonder. Like anyone interested in Wittgenstein, I am fascinated by his life. How I feel about him is quite different from how I feel about Heidegger. He is always the professor, the deep thinker, the great philosopher, and I am always the admiring student of his work. When asked about Aristotle's life, Heidegger replied: "He was born, he thought, he died. The rest is anecdote." A thinker should be judged by what s/he wrote. "Up to a point, Lord Copper," I want to add. I think of Wittgenstein as a human being like myself. But I think of Heidegger, first and last, as a professor, which is how I feel he wanted to be remembered. There is no tension in Heidegger's writings between life and work, but it runs right through Wittgenstein's life. And the last thing he wished to say about it was that it was wonderful.

6

Love and Communication

Some years ago, I committed myself to writing a trilogy; not just three separate and distinct volumes, but a related trinity of books. I had always intended that this final volume should be both a commentary on the first two books, and yet also take their concerns further. Its title, that I came up with back in 2005, was taken from an essay I wrote called "Love and Communication," which was a lengthy and admiring review of John Peters's *Speaking into the Air* (1999). His book's subtitle is "A History of the Idea of Communication," and it starts from the uncontentious proposition that communication emerged as a key concern for us all (not just academics) from the late nineteenth century onward. This is intimately connected with the rise of new technologies of communication from the telegraph to the internet. At the heart of this concern was and is a continuing, still unassuaged anxiety about mediated communication and the ways in which it manipulates and distorts reality and truth. Sincere and genuine, direct and immediate communication seems to be all the more important in the face of the manifold potential of "the media" to bear false witness: interpersonal communication "became thinkable only in the shadow of mediated communication" (Peters 1999: 6). The scandal of mediated "miscommunication" prompted those well-known critiques of mass society and culture, first and most clearly articulated in Weimar Germany by Lukacs and Heidegger in the 1920s and, a decade later, by Adorno and Horkheimer and critical theory (see Scannell 2020 for discussion of this narrative). The liquidation of individuality by impersonal economic, political, and cultural powers was a common theme in the interwar period, shared by intellectuals from opposite ends of the political spectrum. In this scenario, the individual is prey to dark social forces that threaten to overwhelm the lonely integrity of the self.

Transcendent loneliness is a theme that runs through Peters's book and echoes plaintively in its title, *Speaking into the Air*. Is there anyone out there? Or do the winds forlornly blow the words back in one's face? Communicative loneliness takes many forms. The desire for perfect true communication with another, the desire of the living to communicate with the dead, the desire of the human species to get in touch with other species, and, finally, our cosmic anxiety that no life exists outside our small and lonely planet are all wondrously considered: the first in terms of angelic communication, the second in terms of that (to us) bizarre preoccupation with spiritualism of the late nineteenth and early twentieth centuries, the third in terms of thus far vain efforts to communicate with apes, whales, and dolphins, and the fourth in terms of SETI, the Search for Extra-Terrestrial Intelligence. ET has not yet phoned us, even though we would like to believe that he's out there, as Hollywood has imagined on behalf of us all.

Of all these longings, perhaps the most poignant is the desire for perfect union with one another, a true fusion of souls – angelic communication. There is a long tradition of speculation in Christian thought about God's messengers who, now and then (as in the Annunciation), reveal to mortals what He has in mind for them. They are like us but, freed from the corruption of the body, are purely spiritual. The sexuality of angels has been a matter of learned dispute. Are there male and female angels and, if so, what would their sexual union be like? Milton thought that they somehow just co-mingled and tingled for a bit, and John Donne believed that the love of men and women had "just such disparity / As is 'twixt air and angels' purity." Angelic communion is a perfect meeting of minds, the harmony of two hitherto separate souls which have now become one: "Our two souls therefore, which are one, / Though I must go, endure not yet / A breach, but an expansion; / Like gold to airy thinness beat." Something of what Donne's love poetry expressed continues to underpin much modern common-sense thinking about what, *ideally*, love between two people should be like; passion or perfect bodily union as the incarnate expression of the union of souls. Of course, this is not the way we put it nowadays, but the premium we place on sincerity and authenticity in intimate relationships is precisely indicative of our continued longing for "true" communication. Surveys, whether in popular magazines or sociological texts, show that "good communication" is perhaps the most desired quality in modern relationships. There must be no secrets or locked doors between intimates. Each should be fully, genuinely, and sincerely open to the other; truth as mutual self-revelation.

This is the first great variation on the theme of love and communication that runs through the book. The alternative to this, that Peters, in many ways, prefers is nonreciprocal (or one-way) communication. There are moments in the past, he argues, that have an elective affinity with the present. The trick is to spot them and their expressive representatives. The first chapter of *Speaking into the Air* identifies two great variations on the theme of love and communication – dialogue and dissemination – with which the rest of the book will be concerned. The thought of communication can be understood as paradigms of two different ways of human interaction as represented by their illustrious practitioners, Socrates and Jesus. It is part of the book's genius to treat them both as if they were part of our today; not ghostly voices from the dead past, but present and relevant to our concerns. We hear them afresh because that is how Peters hears them. Neither Socrates nor Jesus committed themselves to writing. Our versions of them both are dependent on their followers or disciples: Plato on the one hand, the four gospel writers on the other. What each thought, said, and did, and the differences between them, may serve as "a deep horizon" (Peters 1999: 34) against which to view our contemporary dilemmas in a new light. This is the book's radical historiography. The dead whom it resurrects contribute to a highly original reconfiguration of philosophy, politics, and religion. The dialectic of the written and the spoken, the letter and the spirit, the living and the dead, *logos* and the word made flesh – these fundamental issues remain at the heart of contemporary concern with the *problem* of communication.

We tend, today, to think of dialogue as genuine (real, true) communication because we think it offers, in principle, the possibility of coming to true and mutual understanding. Habermas's influential theory of communicative rationality rests firmly on normative assumptions that he shares with Socrates; the ideal of a cooperative, critical, dialogue oriented toward coming to the best and truest understanding on matters of common concern through the give and take of talk between equals. Socratic dialogue and the Habermasian ideal speech situation are variations on a common theme. Each is underpinned by a faith in relations of presence that guarantee knowledge and truth.

Presence and absence; direct and indirect communication – these are central themes of the *Phaedrus* in which Plato (who wrote it) imagines the older Socrates in conversation with the younger Phaedrus outside the walls of Athens. It is a conversation about speech and writing, love, friendship, and philosophy. It culminates in the famous critique of writing that spells out the motifs of *Speaking into the Air*. Socrates does not like writing because you cannot ask it questions, and for Socrates asking questions was his discourse and his method. Moreover, once something gets written down, it loses all sense of propriety, "reaching indiscriminately those with understanding no less than those who have no business with it, and it doesn't know to whom it should speak and to whom it should not" (Peters 1999: 47). In sum:

Socrates provides a checklist of enduring anxieties that arise in response to transformation in the means of communication. Writing parodies live presence; it is inhuman, lacks interiority, destroys authentic dialogue, is impersonal and cannot acknowledge the individuality of its interlocutors; and it is promiscuous in distribution. Such things have been said about printing, photography, phonography, cinema, radio, television and computers. The great virtue of the *Phaedrus* is to spell out the normative basis of the critique of media in remarkable clarity and, even more, to make us rethink what we mean by *media*. Communication must be soul-to-soul, among embodied live people, in an intimate interaction that is uniquely fit for each participant. (1999: 47)

Then as now love is normatively thought as that which is between two people, alive and present to each other. What passes between them (love as communication: communication as love) is a joining of bodies and a union of souls. Conversation as the art of (mutual) seduction is the prelude to the former. Conversation as philosophy is a prelude to the latter – a marriage of minds. The ideal human relationship is the fusion of both.

The discourse of Jesus and his method stand in sharp contrast with Socrates. Both are exemplified in the parable of the sower; a story with a message told to a large crowd on the shore of the Sea of Galilee. Instead of Socratic one-to-one, two-way communication, we have one-way communication between a single speaker and an anonymous mass of listeners. The story of the sower makes explicit the significance of communication as mass dissemination or *broadcasting*. Before radio gave the word its current meaning, *to broadcast* was an agricultural term for the distribution of seeds abroad. The sower in the parable scatters his seed indiscriminately. Some, as Jesus tells it, fell on stony ground and were pecked up by the birds of the air. Some fell among thorns and were choked as soon as they sprang up. Some fell on shallow soil, grew quickly but soon withered and died. And some fell on fertile ground and yielded a good harvest; thirtyfold, sixtyfold, a hundredfold. It is, of course, a parable about parables – Jesus's own account of his way of spreading the Word.

Socrates, Peters tells us, argued for insemination as being more virtuous than dissemination. Insemination is to implant the seed in another where it will bear fruit. Dissemination is like the sin of Onan who spilled his seed upon the ground. It is a wasteful scatter for there is no guarantee that the seed will, in due course, bear fruit. Put like this, Jesus' method of communication is scandalously inefficient. But that, Peters stunningly argues, is its disinterested kindness and generosity. The parable of the sower makes manifest, in its form as much as its message, that the love of God (*agape*) is indiscriminately available for all, not just the few, the chosen ones, who are open to and receptive of the Word. Broadcasting is a fundamentally democratic form of communication. But more than this, and crucially, it is like the love of God in that it is nonreciprocal. It gives without any expectation of a return. It neither expects nor requires acknowledgment and thanks. The love of God is one way and unconditional and for anyone and everyone anywhere anytime. It *cannot* be reciprocated. Something like this is the blessing of broadcast communication and its indiscriminate scatter.

Miracles

I

I first wrote these pages twenty years ago. And I took Peters's paradigms as a basis for thinking about mediated and unmediated communication, and a justification for public service broadcasting. But *that* now seems a while ago, and broadcasting today is thought of in the academic circles for which I wrote as an exemplar of "old media" and, as such, old hat. Time and the academic field of communication and media studies have moved on. Much has changed since I first floated the idea of a book about love and communication. And though I abide by my initial account of the two paradigms, I would now lay *much* more emphasis on communication as desire: a motif running through *Speaking into the Air*, and this book. The most touching moment in the Still Face Experiment is the little child's utterly spontaneous and immediate joy when her mother reignites their interaction. I now see, much more clearly, that the mother's still face is *not* a human thing. I might say that, in its apparent indifference to her child, the mother's expressionless still face is machine-like (inhuman). The baby's desire is a peculiarly pure expression of human longing for connectivity. Connectivity per se is a deeply felt wish for connection with Others – adult members of human society, not other babies. This longing, or desire, has nothing to do with adult carnal, human love. It is not explained by sociology. It is the deeply felt wish to escape from transcendental loneliness, or solipsism; to leave a world at one with itself and oneself, and enter the world of others.

With Peters, in *Speaking into the Air*, and usually, we think of communication as a human><human interac-

tion. But the two other structures that today's media scholars must think about are human>\<machine interaction and, now, machine>\<machine interaction. I have taken the SFE as the paradigm model of human>\<human interaction. The child, as I see it, is *not* learning language, but is acquiring the multisensory skills of talk with another. To avoid bringing language into the conversation, I prefer *Muttersprache*, which keeps it out. I have argued that language is writing, the original sin and the original technology. In talk, you interact with another human being. With writing, you interact with the page. The puzzle of language is that you cannot *un*imagine it. I am now so comfortable with my own literacy that I cannot imagine a world without it. And I cannot disentangle writing from language, nor myself from human history.

"Did we *invent* human speech?" Wittgenstein once asked himself incredulously, and replied immediately: "No more than we invented walking on two legs" (Kerr 1997: 114). He had a vague, unexamined notion of communication, which he clearly regarded as something *earlier* and more *primitive* than language.

> I want to regard man here as an animal; as a primitive being to which one certainly grants instincts but not *ratiocination*. As a creature in a primitive state. For any *logic* good enough for a *primitive means of communication* needs no apology from us. [Who *is* this "us"? Philosophers? Those of us who have language?] *Language did not emerge from some kind of ratiocination.* (Kerr 1997: 114; emphases added)

"But what," he asks himself, "is the word 'primitive' meant to say here?" to which he responds: "Presumably that the way of behaving is *pre-linguistic*" (Kerr 1997: 114; original emphases). Communicative behavior in human beings is, as we have seen, developmentally prior to entry into a spoken language. The unexamined issue of what Wittgenstein means by *primitive* equates with prehistoric humanity – a talkative (communicative) but preliterate humanity – like other animals *before the invention of writing*. The Zimbabwean musician, Stella Chiweshe, sings of a time when we understood the language of birds and could communicate with them, but that was long ago. Communication today has, for Wittgenstein, a certain kind of logic to it (a logic good enough for the communicative purposes of a primitive animal), but language did not emerge from some (any) kind of communication. He regards communication as more instinctive and primitive than language, and underpinned by a logic which, whatever it is, is not the logic of language. Communication, but not language, is something shared by human beings and other animal species, and the mother–child communicative nexus is the same for human and certain sociable nonhuman mammals.

Wittgenstein denies primitives ratiocination. Presumably then, if we met one, we would not understand her or him (like Chiweshe's birds). But I have tried to show that there are two rationalities: the reasoning capacity and capability of Gricean logic, and the ratiocination of Wittgensteinian logic. The three communicative relationships – human><human, human><machine, machine><machine – correspond with three worlds: the world of *Muttersprache* and communication, the world of writing and language, and the world of Turing machines (of mathematics and science).

Gricean logic underpins communication (talk), while Wittgensteinian logic underpins the written languages of humans and Turing machines. If we can go back in time for a moment, let us take Raymond Williams's tripartite model of culture: in any time now (the present), there is the dominant culture of the day, the residual culture of the vanishing past, and the emergent culture that is coming into existence. These are proxies for the three worlds, W_1, W_2, and W_3, which, for the sake of convenience, are God's world, the human world of today, and, lastly, the machine world. We are still in a W_2 human world. Yet this world is finely balanced between letting go completely of God's world, and inclining more and more to the machine/human world of the present><future.

II

At the start of the postwar epoch, German philosopher Karl Jaspers foresaw that we (historical humanity) were heading into a new axial age (Jaspers 1953). An axial age is a time of transition, a breakout from the present-past and a breakthrough into the present-future. Jaspers believed that the first axial age occurred some two millennia ago when, in quite different parts of the world, new ways of thinking appeared in philosophy and religion that formed the basis of the knowable world that endured until the twentieth century. In the aftermath of the first high-tech, global war we (i.e., West European intellectuals) were pivoting away from the known world of the present><past, and into a different world of the future. The change was from a world under the eye of God (and the world religions were formed in the first

axial age) into a world in which we were under the eye of science and technology (Jaspers 1953: 81–230). Every generation thinks that it is living in new times, but the digital switch-over from the old analogue world in the second half of the last century looks like a decisive, pivotal event. Hitherto in recorded history, human beings, as writing and language developed, created more and more machines that enabled growing numbers of people to lead lives increasingly freed from necessity. But always, the machine was no more than a servant (however more efficient) of its master, humankind. What Turing discovered broke with this. He invented *thinking* machines that were independent of human beings and, though originally tasked by human programmers, could interact with and learn from other like-minded machines. The question for the future is whether we are stumbling toward a world more and more defined by Turing machines.

I don't like this kind of portentous stuff, and I'm not in the business of prophecy. I'm just saying. Or to put it another way, I belong to the past, not the future. The difficult thing, in getting started, is, as Wittgenstein pointed out, showing the road to be taken, and following it through to its end. (Heidegger thought along similar hodological lines.) There comes a point when you just have to stop, and I am very nearly there. I am myself a child of the twentieth century. It is not that I prefer to live in the past, rather than the present, but the world today is no longer the one in which I grew up. There is neither sentimentality nor nostalgia in recalling that then God was in His heaven, and I was a Catholic, and I went to school, and had a guardian angel. To say now that I stand in need of forgiveness is not like saying sorry to God. It is to acknowledge Him.

Acknowledgment is, in its usual sense, the recognition of the (human) Other. I remember, from historical romances I read long ago, that the worst thing you could do "in polite society" was to ignore someone deliberately. So, you might be walking down the street and see someone you knew coming toward you. The "polite" thing to do is to say "hello," and if you pass by in silence it might be interpreted (via Gricean logic) as a "cut," a deliberate, and heinous, insult. Duels were fought, and men died, for lack of acknowledgment. You might say that the mother momentarily "cuts" her little child when she goes stone-faced on her. Stanley Cavell writes that "the ability to praise guards against the threat of skepticism." He goes on to ask: "What is it about praise that it should emerge as an essential topic of the examination of our acknowledgment of others?" (2005: 5). It is, in an entirely ordinary sense, a momentary act of recognition of other human beings, as in the acknowledgments that go at the start of books or PhDs, or in the long list of credits at the end of the movie.

III

My communicative longing is not for Peters's communion of souls but for a world in which God is in His heaven, and thus all's well with us mortals who dwell below on middle-earth. But I no longer live in His presence. And the past, like the dead, will not return. God has disappeared into the wings of history. Putting Him under erasure means at one and the same time that I cannot do without Him but He, alas, is no longer in place up there, in the wholly human world in which I live. When I was a child, I was taught that the three theological virtues were faith, hope, and charity. They are so called, in Catholic doctrine, as the gifts, freely bestowed on us, by God's grace. I was touched, on a visit to Italy, to see them represented as angels hovering above the virtuous and wise ruler in the marvelous allegorical frescos of *Good and Bad Government* by Ambrogio Lorenzetti in one of the great rooms of the Palazzo Pubblico that towers over the beautiful shell-shaped campo at the heart of the Tuscan city of Siena. I found myself reflecting on how well they understood, in medieval Italy, the relationship between religion and politics, expressed, in so many ways, in the art and architecture of the place. The town's great religious building, its Duomo, is in its own and separate space from the Campo and Palazzo. It is said that the towers of the cathedral and the palace were built to exactly the same height so that neither should appear to dominate the other.

These three things abide – faith, hope, and love. But the greatest of them is love. So wrote St. Paul to the Christian community in Corinth. Everyone knows these words, and they remain true to this day. They stand in an integral relationship to each other: faith and hope go together, with faith first; and underpinning them both is trust. We might put it as an algorithm: $f + h/t = love$. This, in other words, is the care structure. As a rule, we wake up every morning expecting that the day will be an ordinary one in which we will do what we must, meet and talk with others, go about our affairs, and accomplish all this without undue complications. That life goes on as usual without our even noticing it is the gift of the hidden care structures that hold the world in place through time; that produce and reproduce it as a working, workable, workaday world and, in so doing, guarantee our ease of being in it.

Once upon a time, faith, hope, and trust appeared as God's gifts to humanity. I am not saying this. Nor am I denying it. I do think, though, that Wittgenstein's experience of absolute safety (in the hands of God) turns out to be the same as Heidegger's care structure.[11] That is to say, trust in God and trust in the care structure are the same thing – an absolute, an unconditional thing. I feel safe in God's hands. I feel safe in the ordinary, everyday world. Wittgenstein's notion of absolute safety is a childlike thing. I have a very distant memory of myself as a sleeping little child in the back of the car. And when we got home, I was lifted out by one of my parents (I don't know which) and in that moment I felt supremely safe, supremely happy. Nothing could go wrong. Nothing could hurt me. It is not like the other two experiences that Wittgenstein discusses: the wonder of the world, and absolute guilt. I'm sure that these are part of his adult life. But absolute safety is more like a longing, a desire for something lost, that he had as a child but no longer. Certainly it is how I understand my Catholic childhood.

Wittgenstein and Heidegger were born in the same year (one in Austria, the other in Germany); they both had Catholic childhoods and became world renowned for their academic work. Their philosophies are very different, and yet I feel they touch each other at the same point. Being safe in God's hands and being at home in the world *are* the same thing, though differently expressed. The care structure was and is made by human beings to create a world as a fit place in which to live and lead one's usual life. Imagine if it were

---

[11]I am deeply grateful to my friend, Tarik Sabry, for pointing this out to me.

otherwise. Imagine a monstrous world in which, for instance, nothing worked (easily, effortlessly). The car works sometimes and not others. And likewise, the TV set, the washing machine, etc., etc. Marx thought that what was hidden in humanly made things was exploited human labor. I think so too. But I would also add that the care structure is equally hidden in every humanly made thing. It is not an either/or. Alienated labor *or* the care structure. *Both* are true. In an utterly thoughtless, but necessary, way, the consumer goods of the consumer society are always the same, and always perfect: $f + h/t$ is inbuilt into everything. And this is so because the care structure is immanent in human beings, as it is in the human world. The little algorithm of love can be understood either way; as a divine gift, or as the human care structure. I can no longer experience my being in the world as the former, because I no longer live in God's world. He may be disappearing from the historical world in which I live, but I feel His presence in Heidegger's *Being and Time*.

Finis

Coda

I have been wondering, while writing this book, who it is *for*. Let me say straightaway that it is *not* for me. It is not a memoir, nothing at all like recollections in tranquility, none of the grand-old-man stuff, offering pearls of wisdom (based on a lifetime's experience, blah blah) for future generations. Nor am I (though I was stubbornly addicted to this delusion) trying to write "like a human being with claims upon the attention of other human beings like myself." Whenever I drew upon my earlier "personal," life I did so to make a point, to illustrate something. The personal is quite impersonal. I presuppose, as Wittgenstein does, that my experiences have a for-anyone-as-someone structure (Scannell 2000). We all have them, and they are, in certain respects, uniquely mine. But anyone and everyone I suppose has wondered at the wonder of existence at some time or other. Experience is a fore-given thing – one of those things that distinguish us from machines. It is no longer a question of what distinguishes us from nonhuman animals.

That said, this is for present and future generations

of scholars studying communication and media as much
as any informed lay public. It is no more than a small
offering; an attempt at self-clarification that may be
useful for others who struggle with the existential dilemmas thrown up in trying to think about and understand
the questions that are implicated in "communication,"
and "media." Here are a couple of further thoughts for
now – "now" being a doubled temporality: the time of
history, and the time of lifetime, and both in the same-
time-now, the living present. Their intersection is what
produces historical change. Heidegger thought of the
usual human as being-toward-death. But the question
of mortality is only half of it. Natality is just as, if not
more, important. The birth of any and every child comes
charged with messianic promise: that *this* child might
make all the difference in the world. Life and death
presuppose each other; their dialectic yields historical
continuity and change. As usual adults, we struggle on
in our working lives, hoping to add to the collective
depth of experience and knowledge that constitutes our
academic field. And I have found myself trying to look
more carefully at talk and writing, immediate and medi-
ate forms of communication. To do this I began with
birth. And this was not in any way a self-conscious
thing, and I have only just now, as I write this, seen
that I was drawn both to beginnings *and* endings in this
book.

Just one last thought. It is no longer possible to take
the infrastructure of self and world for granted. The historical human world looks forward and back; back to
the connections between God's world and this, and forward to our future world, the wholly human><machine,
machine><human world. First things first. I would sug-

gest myself that the difference between human><human and human><machine interactions could be expressed as follows. A communicative interaction takes place between humans, and their machines when humans come first. When humans come second, the nature of the interaction is defined by the machine in the first place, and is a transactional, rather than a communicative interaction. The differences between communication and transaction point up the differences between humans and machines, and how they interconnect with each other. Broadcast radio and television will continue to uphold this distinction.

References

Annan, N. (1955) "The intellectual aristocracy," in J. H. Plumb (ed.), *Studies in Social History*. London: Longman.

Bonner, F. (2003) *Ordinary Television. Analysing Popular TV*. London: Sage.

Braver, L. (2015) *Division III of Heidegger's Being and Time*. Cambridge, MA: MIT Press.

Buscombe, E. (1975) *Football on Television*. London: British Film Institute.

Cavell, S. (2005) *Philosophy the Day after Tomorrow*. Cambridge, MA: Harvard University Press.

Copeland, B. J. (ed.) (2004) *The Essential Turing*. Oxford: Oxford University Press.

Derrida, J. (1976) *Of Grammatology*. Baltimore, MD: Johns Hopkins University Press.

Dreyfus, H. (1991) *Being-in-the-World*. Cambridge, MA: MIT Press.

Figal, G. (2009) *The Heidegger Reader*. Bloomington: Indiana University Press.

References

Garfinkel, H. (1984 [1967]) *Studies in Ethnomethodology*. Cambridge: Polity.

Grice, H. P. (1989) *Studies in the Way of Words*. Cambridge, MA: Harvard University Press.

Heidegger, M. (1962) *Being and Time*. Oxford: Blackwell.

Heidegger, M. (1992 [1924]) *The Concept of Time*. Oxford: Blackwell.

Heidegger, M. (1999 [1923]) *Ontology: The Hermeneutics of Facticity*. Bloomington: Indiana University Press.

Hodges, A. (2012) *Alan Turing: The Enigma*. London: Vintage Books.

Innis, H. (1950) *Empire and Communication*. Oxford: Oxford University Press.

Innis, H. (1964 [1951]) *The Bias of Communication*. Toronto: Toronto University Press.

Jaspers, K. (1953) *The Origin and Goal of History*. London: Routledge.

Kanterian, E. (2007) *Ludwig Wittgenstein*. London: Reaktion Books.

Kerr, K. (1997) *Theology After Wittgenstein*. London: S.P.C.K.

Knausgaard, K. O. (2004) *A Time for Everything*. New York: Archipelago Books.

Laslett, P. (1983 [1965]) *The World We Have Lost – Further Explored*, 3rd edn. London: Routledge.

Malloch, S., and Trevarthen, C. (eds.) (2009) *Communicative Musicality: Exploring the Basis of Human Companionship*. Cambridge: Cambridge University Press.

McLuhan, M. (2011 [1962]) *The Gutenberg Galaxy*. Toronto: Toronto University Press.

McLuhan, M. (1964) *Understanding Media*. New York: McGraw Hill.

Mesman, J., Ijzendoorn, M., and Bakermans-Kranenburg, M. (2009) "The many faces of the Still-Face Paradigm: A review and meta-analysis," *Developmental Review* 30(2): 120–162.

Monk, R. (1991) *Ludwig Wittgenstein: The Duty of Genius*. London: Vintage Books.

Pattison, G. (2000) *The Later Heidegger*. London: Routledge.

Peters, J. D. (1999) *Speaking into the Air: A History of the Idea of Communication*. Chicago, IL: Chicago University Press.

Peters, J. D. (2015) *The Marvelous Clouds*. Chicago, IL: Chicago University Press.

Powers, N., and Trewarthen, C. (2009) "Voices of shared emotion and meaning: Young infants and their mothers in Scotland and Japan," in S. Malloch and C. Trevarthen (eds.), *Communicative Musicality: Exploring the Basis of Human Companionship*. Cambridge: Cambridge University Press, pp. 209–240.

Safranski, R. (1998) *Martin Heidegger: Between Good and Evil*. Cambridge, MA: Harvard University Press.

Scannell, P. (1991) *Broadcast Talk*. London: Sage.

Scannell, P. (2000) "For anyone-as-someone structures," *Media, Culture & Society* 22(4): 5–24.

Scannell, P. (2005) "Love and communication," *Media, Culture & Society* 27(4): 614–621.

Scannell, P. (2009) "The question concerning technology," in M. Bailey (ed.), *Narrating Media History*. London: Routledge, pp. 199–211.

References

Scannell, P. (2014) *Television and the Meaning of "Live"*. Cambridge: Polity.

Scannell, P. (2019) *Why Do People Sing?* Cambridge: Polity.

Scannell, P. (2020 [2007]) *Media and Communication*. London: Sage.

Scannell, P., and Cardiff, D. (1991) *A Social History of British Broadcasting, 1922–1939*. Oxford: Blackwell.

Shattuck, R. (1980) *The Forbidden Experiment: The Story of the Wild Boy of Aveyron*. New York: Farrar Straus Giroux.

Singer, P. (1995 [1975]) *Animal Liberation*, 2nd edn. London: Pimlico.

Williams, R. (1974) *Television: Technology and Cultural Form*. London: Methuen.

Winston, B. (1998) *Media, Technology & Society: A History from the Telegraph to the Internet*. London: Routledge.

Wittgenstein, L. (1969) *On Certainty*. Oxford: Blackwell.

Wittgenstein, L. (1984) *Culture and Value*, ed. G. H. von Wright, trans. P. Winch. Chicago, IL: Chicago University Press.

Wittgenstein, L. (2014 [1922]) *Tractatus Logico-Philosophicus*. London: Routledge Great Minds.

Zamuner, E., Valentina Di Lascio, E., and Levy, D. (eds.) (2007) *Lecture on Ethics, Ludwig Wittgenstein*. Macerata: Quodlibet società cooperativa.